I SAW OUR LADY

Tom Neary.

'Blessed are the poor in spirit, for theirs is the kingdom of heaven.

'Blessed are those who mourn, for they shall be comforted.

'Blessed are the meek, for they shall inherit the earth.

'Blessed are those who hunger and thirst for righteousness,
for they shall be satisfied.

'Blessed are the merciful, for they shall obtain mercy.

'Blessed are the pure in heart, for they shall see God.

'Blessed are the peacemakers, for they shall be called sons of God.

'Blessed are those who are persecuted for righteousness' sake,
for theirs is the kingdom of heaven.

'Blessed are you when men revile you and persecute you and utter all
kinds of evil against you falsely on my account.

Rejoice and be glad, for your reward is great in heaven.'
(Matt. 5:1–12)

Dedication

**To the visionaries of Knock -
the poor and humble children of Mary.**

ISBN 0-9515807-1-X

Fifth Edition - October, 1995.
©Tom Neary, 1977.

Published by the Custodians of Knock Shrine,
Co. Mayo, Ireland.

Origination & Printing by
Cashin Printing Services Ltd.,
Castlebar, Co. Mayo

I SAW OUR LADY

Tom Neary.

Contents

Foreword

It is with a feeling of deep humility that I write a foreword to this updated edition of Tom Neary's book. The Preface which follows this, was written by my beloved predecessor, Monsignor James Horan, who over a span of twenty-three years developed Knock into what it is today, one of the leading Marian Shrines of the world.

The greatest tribute I can pay to Tom Neary is to state that, during all those years, he was one of Monsignor Horan's right-hand men. Tom is an authority on Knock Shrine, its history, its development, its problems, as well as its glories. I thank him for the many years he has given to Knock and for the leadership and example he has given as head-Steward. This book is but one example of his many contributions to Knock Shrine. Any reader who is interested in the story of Knock Shrine will also feel grateful to him when they read this book.

Dominick Grealy,

1st May, 1989.

Preface

At about 8 o'clock on the memorable evening of August 21st, 1879, Our Lady, St. Joseph and St. John the Evangelist appeared at the south gable of the church at Knock; beside them and a little to the right was an altar with a cross and the figure of a lamb. The Apparition was seen by fifteen people, young and old, who watched it for two hours in pouring rain and recited the Rosary. Most Rev. Dr. John MacHale, Archbishop of Tuam, only six weeks after the Apparition, set up a Commission of Inquiry which reported that the "testimony of all taken as a whole, was trustworthy and satisfactory".

Archbishop Gilmartin set up a Commission in 1936 to examine the three surviving witnesses of the Apparition: Mrs. Mary O'Connell (Mary Byrne), Patrick Byrne and John Curry. All three confirmed their original statement in 1879. Mrs. O'Connell gave evidence under oath from her death bed and at the end of her statement she added; "I am quite clear about everything I have said, and I make this statement knowing I am going before my God".

I have just given you the official account of the Apparition at Knock. However, I always thought it would be wonderful to read the accounts given by newspaper correspondents of the Apparition itself and the early pilgrimages. For that reason I had some research done in the National Library, Dublin, and I got photostat copies of newspaper articles on Knock from English and Irish newspapers. I found these features so interesting and so fascinating that I asked Mr. Tom Neary to edit them and put them in book form. He has done an excellent job and has produced a most interesting book and I recommend it to all pilgrims.

James Horan P.P.

14th April, 1977.

Good tidings of Great Joy":
The Apparition Evening at Knock - Thursday, August 21st 1879.

AUTHOR'S NOTE

As this book deals essentially with the first year of Knock's history as a shrine, namely 1879—1880, the author wishes it to be known that it has been largely researched and compiled from the various newspapers of that period.

The following newspapers of note have been included in the research material:

"The Nation"
"The Freeman's Journal"
"The Weekly News"
"The Irish Times"
"The Daily Express'"
"The Daily Telegraph"
"The Cork Examiner"
"The Limerick Reporter and Tipperary Vindicator"
"The Ballinrobe Chronicle and Mayo Advertiser"
"The Connaught Telegraph"
"The Mayo Examiner"
"The Galway Vindicator and Connaught Advertiser"
"The Tuam News"
"The Roscommon Journal and Western Reporter".

Tom Neary

BLACK CENTURIES

Black
Centuries of desolation and pain.
Bloodstained fields of our frozen dead,
Fruits of enemy labours.
A suppressed race,
Mourning.

Priest and peasant hunted—
The Mass Rock.
Persecution.

Landlord might holding sway.
Tenant blight.
Desperation undescribed.
Cabin bashing
Bursting,
Burning.
Women wailing with their children,
By the Way.

Long lean hungry years,
Withered skeletons of humanity.
Starvation.

Mary's prayer—
The Crown of Roses—
Only hope
By hearth and hedgerow.
Faith in their maker,
The sole strength of
Patrick's orphans.
Voices crying in the wilderness.
Thy kingdom come.
Thy will be done

What meaning this?
A purifying?
Preparation?
A cross before the crown?
Doubtless
Heaven's choicest gifts are won.
Then sorrow's wane,
Before
The blazing glory of the dawn.

TOM NEARY

An eviction scene: The battering ram at work

CHAPTER 1

Mary visits Mayo's hill country

Knock, sanctuary of faith, hope and love!

There are on the earth a number of favoured spots, where the mercy of God is manifested with a sort of prodigality.

These blessed places are called sanctuaries—that is to say, places specially sanctified and sanctifying.

The good God, in order to satisfy the wants of his heart and to revive unceasingly our faith and confidence, deigns to manifest to and inundate us with the treasures of his love.

For this purpose he chooses certain places, which thus become meeting-places of prayer, of piety, of adoration, where the faithful acquire new strength and poor sinners are more easily converted and reconciled.

Always in these sanctuaries the divine grace flows more abundantly than elsewhere, like the smoke of a volcano which never ceases; and often, whether for the consolation of the good, for the conversion or for the confusion of sinners, the almighty mercy of God there manifests itself by apparitions, by sudden cures, and by other miracles and prodigies of a supernatural kind.

Knock is one of these sanctuaries of faith, hope and love, not only to-day but from its origin.

Heaven has marked her with an evangelical atmosphere ever since the Apparition of August 21st, 1879.

The story of Knock is at once the story of a heavenly vision and the story of its humble seers—an Irish Visitation.

It is marvellous in its simplicity, extraordinary only in its ordinariness.

All in this unique story unfolds in the translucent light of the "Beatitudes". Read them well for therein you will find the reasons why Knock has been honoured with a visit from the mother of our Lord.

A bit of heaven descends from the skies and glorifies Knock, for there, is purity and poverty, meekness and humility, echoes of Nazareth.

If I had to compare the event of Knock to some evangelic scene, I should willingly choose in Saint Luke, the following passage:

"Mary set out and went as quickly as she could to a town in the hill country of Judah. She went into Zechariah's house and greeted Elizabeth. Now as soon as Elizabeth heard Mary's greeting, the child leapt in her womb and Elizabeth was filled with the Holy Spirit. She gave a loud cry and said, 'Of all women you are the most blessed, and blessed is the fruit of your womb. Why should I be honoured with a visit from the mother of my Lord? For the moment your greeting reached my ears, the child in my womb leapt for joy. Yes, blessed is she who believed that the promise made her by the Lord would be fulfilled.' And Mary said,

"My soul proclaims the greatness of the Lord
and my spirit exults in God my Saviour;
because he has looked upon his lowly handmaid.
Yes, from this day forward all generations will call me Blessed,
For the Almighty has done great things for me.
Holy is his name,
and his mercy reaches from age to age for those who fear him.
He has shown the power of his arm,
He has routed the proud of heart.
He has pulled down princes from their thrones and exalted the lowly.
The hungry he has filled with good things,
The rich sent empty away.
He has come to the help of Israel his servant,
mindful of his mercy.
-according to the promise he made to our ancestors-
of His mercy to Abraham and to His descendants for ever."
Mary stayed with Elizabeth about three months and then went back home.

This beautiful extract from the Gospel of St. Luke tells of the Visitation. The story of Knock is also the story of a visitation. Mary comes to visit her Irish children in the hill country of Mayo, and so in a sense, it too has become a land of the Gospel.

Within these pages is unfolded something of that visitation and something of its aftermath.

In order that the atmosphere of both may be captured for the reader, what is written herein is based upon the accounts of eye-witnesses.

Chief amongst these are the accounts of the visionaries themselves—the chosen children of Mary.

Here too are accounts based upon the reports of the leading journalists of the day who set down, in the national and provincial newspapers, a full and faithful account of all that was important.

Insofar as is possible, the narrative is in 'the first person' and 'the historic present' so that the humble origins which have made and shaped

Knock—now a leading world shrine of Mary—may be made present, once again, to us, more than one hundred years later.

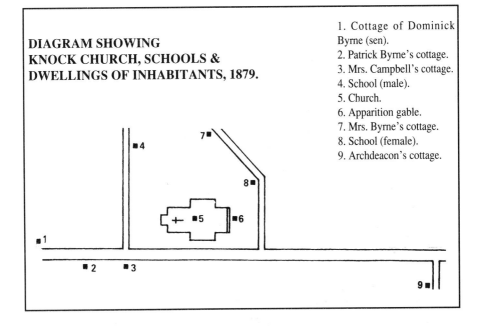

**DIAGRAM SHOWING
KNOCK CHURCH, SCHOOLS &
DWELLINGS OF INHABITANTS, 1879.**

1. Cottage of Dominick Byrne (sen).
2. Patrick Byrne's cottage.
3. Mrs. Campbell's cottage.
4. School (male).
5. Church.
6. Apparition gable.
7. Mrs. Byrne's cottage.
8. School (female).
9. Archdeacon's cottage.

The village of Knock at the time of the Apparition.

THE FAMINE SPECTRE

'Tis around us and about us,
　'Tis with us everywhere,
We can feel its dark wings beating
　On the still and frightened air.
Tho we see it not nor hear it,
　It is there—we know it—still,
The famine spectre waiting
　And seeking whom to kill.

Grim of aspect is the spectre,
　Fixed his eyes and flaming stand,
A shroud for his only garment
　Held tight in his skinny hand.
As to his full height uprising
　He breathes on the air a breath
That is poison to all it touches,
And to all that inhale it, death.
ANON.

He swept our moor and mountain,
　With a giant stride amain,
Pausing only for a moment
　To rest, and then on again.
And tho' men see not nor hear him,
　Well they know that he is there;
For they feel his accursed presence
　In the still and frightened air.

On the road what figures pass you,
　With a sigh that is like a wail,
Sunken eyes, cheeks seared and hollow,
　And lips tight drawn and pale,
Scarce able with pain and weakness
　To drag their tired limbs along—
That were once clear bright-eyed women,
　And stalwart men and strong!

Published in "The Cork Examiner", Saturday, February 28th, 1880.

A Picture of Poverty: **"Widow and dying Child."** *"The Graphic"* London 1879.

CHAPTER 2

Who Can Withhold a Helping Hand?

In this chapter, the reader is brought face to face with the misery, poverty and hopelessness of the people of the West of Ireland, at the time when Mary the Mother of God comes from heaven, to console and strengthen her children. They are in dire need of a helping hand. They need some hope to cling to.

The Mother of God does not turn away from her dearly loved sons and daughters in their hour of need. No, rather does she come to help, because she is such a good and caring mother. She wishes to share their sufferings, their crosses, their miseries, just as she did for all mankind on Calvary.

A special correspondent of "The Daily Telegraph" visits the Ballina district of Co. Mayo, and is shown around by a Fr. Conway. He writes a report in Ballina on January 4th, 1880 which is carried in his own newspaper and also in "The Nation" and "The Weekly News". The following is based upon this report which is entitled "An Englishman's Revelations":

It is unique, as far as my observation goes, to approach the homes of small tenant farmers each surrounded by its ten, or fifteen or twenty acres, with geese and poultry in the yard, and other tokens of well-doing, and then to find on entering that the people, short of killing their egg-layers, do not know where to look for the next meal.

This, let me say emphatically, is the peculiar form of distress with which we have now to do.

You might travel from one end of the country to the other and scarcely suspect its existence, for it never obtrudes; but it is there all the same, and crushing thousands of decent, respectable people in its grasp.

First of all Fr. Conway shows me the state to which men are reduced who are merely day-labourers and hold no land.

For day labourers there is, amid the general stagnation, absolutely no employment, and in the cabins we visit, the men are found idle at home, watching the sure and certain absorption of their half-bag of Indian meal, beyond which in no case can they see aught of the means of life.

One hut lies off the road, and has to be reached by stepping over a half-ruined wall into a tiny enclosure reeking with rotting straw and manure, gathering there apparently to be sold if luck should bring a buyer.

Passing with care through this unsavoury place, we enter the hut, to find the usual man, woman, and children upon the earthen floor.

In one place, a heap of tiny, half-decayed potatoes; in another, the family bed, which I would rather not describe; on the hearthstone, a miserable smoking heap of odds and ends—for of turf there is none in this district—and all around the unimaginable articles that seem to have a use in such a place.

The sharp but kindly questions of the priest brought out a now familiar story—no work, no store beyond the little heap of potatoes, and no hope.

Yet there is nothing save patient resignation in the look and manner of the father and mother, whose wretched home is lighted up, moreover, by a beautiful little girl, some five or six years old—a child with bright eyes and rosy cheeks and flowing hair, whom many a painter would gladly commit to canvas.

I tempt this lovely albeit ragged and unkempt angel out of the gloom of the bedroom corner with a bit of silver, and she flashes brighter than the coin that is hurriedly carried back into darkness.

I wonder if the rotting heaps outside will ever make the eyes of the little one brighter and her cheeks glow a more fiery red!

Whether or no, the demon of fever cannot be far away.

From the day-labourers' cabins Fr. Conway takes me to the residence of a widow renting 16 acres of land, two of which were last year planted with potatoes, the remainder being planted with grass.

We find the poor soul—a woman in the prime of life, of respectable appearance, and superior manners for her class—absolutely helpless and hopeless.

Her two acres of potatoes have produced nothing; stock she has none; and her grass land, in the probable event of not being sub-let for grazing, is but a dead weight crushing her down.

Payment of rent cannot be thought of, since she has not wherewith to buy a meal, and her cottage would have been fireless but for the help of her brother, who comes a long distance over the hills to cut such wood as he can find about the place.

Thus without means, without credit and without prospect of retrieving bad fortune, she and her family are drifting on, from day to day, till it shall please the landlord to turn them out.

In another place, we find a man renting a rood of land, and, being therefore ineligible for outdoor relief, destitute of employment, food, and the wherewithal to plant his little plot in hope of better luck.

But perhaps the worst case is that of a farmer to whom Fr. Conway takes me by way of climax.

This man pays, or is expected to pay an annual rental of £31; his house and premises are kept in decent order; and, altogether, he is a very favourable specimen of the Irish tenant. Yet he has not, through utter failure of crops, been able to pay his rent, beyond £5 worth of hay which his landlord's wife bought not long ago, and told him to set against his debt.

More than this, he assures me that, were his whole possessions sold, they would not defray one quarter of the liabilities necessitated by bad seasons.

Still more, he and his family are at this moment living upon Indian meal, payment for which has been guaranteed by the good parish priest.

In yet another case, a man, his wife, and seven children are found penniless with no claim on the poor-rate, crushed by a load of debt, and having their only hope in a loan from America, for which Fr. Conway has become security.

I shall add nothing to these deplorable facts save a word of thanks to Fr. Conway for enabling me to make them known, as typical of the destitution setting in over all these Western lands.

In view of them, who can wonder at fervid or even unreasoning eloquence, or who can withhold a helping hand?

In the month of January, 1880 the same correspondent comes to Westport, Co. Mayo to observe the actual conditions under which the people are living. He wishes to see for himself, what the position is, in the deep West. He confines his investigation to the area around Croagh Patrick and a local man, who knows the locality well, accompanies him, and acts as his guide.

When he has visited the scenes of poverty, he returns to Westport where he writes a detailed account of what he has seen.

The account which follows is based upon this report which is published in all the aforementioned newspapers in January, 1880:

From Murrisk my guide takes me along a by-road into the mountains, and to a cabin where lives a family of six sons and a daughter, all dependent upon the eldest, a young fellow of nineteen.

I pity this lad from my heart of hearts. Both parents are dead and he galantly stands by his brothers and sister—who are too young to do anything for themselves—rather than permit them to enter the workhouse.

He farms two acres of land, has paid no rent, can find no employment, and is dependent upon casual circumstances for a daily meal of stirabout.

Now let me sketch two scenes, at sight of which the least sympathetic reader will cry "Hold, enough", and with these I shall conclude.

Going down the road leading to the "barrier" I notice before me a ruined cottage, against the front wall of which is a heap of refuse, piled up as I conceive, after a careless glance from a little distance, with curious irregularities of outline. I take no further notice, but good Heavens! when I approach, the "irregularities" begin to stir. Those little heaps on the top of the great heap are not refuse, but a mother and three children taking the air outside their dwelling.

From broken wall to broken wall, over as much of the area as would make a pigstye, they have placed pieces of wood interlaced with straw and furze, and underneath this they creep when they "go home".

At present they are on the dunghill outside, crouching there silent and motionless, the woman looking straight before her into vacancy, and refusing a word even to a kindly question.

The boy answers, abruptly, that his father is "down there" and that is all.

I do not look into the "home".

The open area of the cottage is unutterably filthy, and I turn away sick.

Now for my second scene.

I am directed to a cabin so dilapidated that, but for a volume of smoke pouring through the door, I should have supposed it tenantless.

I am asked to enter, and do so by an aperture not much more than 4 feet high.   At first the acrid vapour blinds my eyes with tears—fit tribute to the genius of the place—but in a little while I am able to look around.

Then the involuntary exclamation, "Good God!" bursts from me.

In this most miserable den, a few feet square, with the roof open here and there to the sky, and propped by timber, down which water is trickling to the muddy floor—in this place, with no furniture to speak of, and dark for lack of a window, save when lit by a spluttering fire of branches, live a man, his wife, six children, and the wife's aged father and mother.

And here they are, all of them, filling the cabin so that there is scarcely room for myself and my companion.

But what are the children—some of whom wear only a single garment—doing on the floor by the hearth?

See, they have in their midst a bowl of Indian meal, and are feeding themselves from it, while a starved cat, mewing piteously, strives to gain an entrance within the circle.

"That is all they'll ate the day, the crayturs," said the father.

I can stand this no longer, and giving a trifle, in return for which I receive a host of blessings, I leave the place.

Our final account of poverty in the West of Ireland is based on a report written by our "Daily Telegraph" friend, in Clifden, Co. Galway, on January 10th, 1880. The day is a Saturday and the correspondent has just returned to the capital of West Connaught after seeing for himself the wretchedness of the poor of Connemara.

His guide has been the local priest, Fr. Flannery, who has an intimate knowledge of the entire district.

The correspondent's report appears in the columns of "The Daily Telegraph", "The Nation" and "The Weekly News":

Fr. Flannery's car rattles me over a wretched by-road to a place called Emlaghmore, and to an illustration of the tenacity with which the Connemara peasant sticks to a holding of some sort, even if it be no larger than the earth covered by a bee-hive.

By the side of the road, on a patch of waste, is a mound of soil and rubbish, such as one often sees about the premises of an untidy farmer; close to it stands a bench and a few articles of domestic utility, and from the base of the mound rises a little column of smoke.

This is the residence of a man whom, some time ago, the landlord evicted, and who stands there, towering far above his present habitation, to tell me as much of the fact as I cared to know.

Under like circumstances an English peasant would probably have betaken himself to the workhouse, but the Irishman squats by the wayside and has built with mud and sticks and rubbish this strange abode.

Looking at the place I hardly believe myself in a civilised country, nor when a head emerges from the hole out of which smoke is pouring can I resist an impression that it will be followed by the body of a savage. But both head and body belong to an Irishwoman, and after her comes crawling out an Irish child.

Stooping down I look through the aperture and see a fire and a lot of litter, the fire being the sole indication that the den is other than the lair of an animal.

Hence we drive to the shore, and giving the car in charge of a man idling there—all the men of this region are idling, alas!—we roam among the sand hillocks in search of something.

Presently Fr. Flannery cries, "Here it is!" and points to a hole in the bank partly stopped by a lobster-pot.

Looking in, we see, as well as gathering darkness allowed, that a cave has been excavated and is used as a dwelling, on the floor being the ashes of an extinct fire, while on ascending the bank, we find an aperture in the earth through which smoke has evidently long made its upward way.

This is, indeed, the residence of another of Queen Victoria's subjects, and to this, unless something be speedily done will many another come.

Rents cannot be paid while there is nothing to be earned and when evictions abound, as they threaten to abound, we shall hear that scores of families are living, or dying in "dens and caves of the earth".

Such a prospect as this is in harmony with the scene as we drive back in the early night through far-stretching wastes of rocky soil, past miserable hovels, under the black sky, and to the music of a moaning wind from the "melancholy ocean".

With such poverty on all sides, it is not surprising that those who can drag themselves away from their loved ones and who may have the wherewithal to travel are leaving the country. The exodus is not confined to the deep West entirely. It has spread like a disease across our land.

The narrative which follows is based upon a report of emigration which appears in "The Galway Vindicator and Connaught Advertiser" of Wednesday, May 19th, 1880:

In fact the emigration from the ports of Ireland continues at a most extraordinary rate.

Today, 250 fine healthy young men and women, ranging in age from 19 to 26, left Belfast by special train on the Northern Counties Railway for Larne, where they embarked on board the steamship "State of Alabama" for New York.

The stream of emigration from Ulster has been very great during the past weeks.

The "State of Alabama" had on board to-day some 700 passengers all told, and the State Line last week 800. On an average 200 emigrants leave Larne weekly by these steamers, which call at that port every Saturday on their outward voyage.

Hundreds take their departure every week by the cross-Channel steamers for Liverpool and Glasgow en route to America.

"**A friendly visit: No work; no credit**" *"The Graphic"*, - London 1879

UNEMPLOYED

In the lone and silent market place
  The labourer waiting stands,
Gazing in numb bewilderment
  At the spade in his idle hands.
Sunken his cheek and dulled his eye,
  And upon his patient face
Stand out in relief, the woeful lines
  That care and hunger trace.

Silent and lone is the market-place;
  No bustle or busy hum.
No merry laugh of the country folks,
  But a void and silence dumb.
No buyers and sellers crowding in
  For traffic—but instead,
One only cry it re-echoes now—
The cry of the poor for bread.

The labourer raises his patient eyes
  And sadly gazes round,
Hoping for aught, he scarce knows what,
  Watching for sight or sound.
And again to earth he drops his eyes,
  With a little sigh of pain;
For none cometh to hire those willing hands
  That are pleading for work in vain.

In the lone and silent market-place
  Behold him waiting yet,
In his sunken eyes despair's dull gleam.
  His teeth in hunger set.
O ye, that have wealth and pride of place
  And station and swelling lands,
Come forward, give food to the weakened frame
  Give work to the willing hands!

E . L. H. Skibbereen .

Published in Supplement to "The Cork Examiner",
Saturday, February 21st, 1880

19.

CHAPTER 3

Multitudes and Miracles

The accounts in this chapter are based upon the report of a correspondent writing for "The Tuam News" in January, 1880. His report appears in the paper dated Friday, Jan. 23rd of that year.

A copy of this report is also carried by "The Limerick Reporter and Tipperary Vindicator" and the date of the edition is Tuesday Evening, January 27th, 1880:

A wonderful centre of religious fervour and a great incentive to faith is suddenly starting into form and favour in South Mayo.

At present the West of Ireland is the trysting-place of all who are labouring for the improvement of the condition of the small farmers living on Irish soil.

The eyes of all in England, and of friends and foes to the cause of the people at home and abroad, are turned to the West of Ireland.

It is there a flame of political and social fervour is being fanned which is spreading at present all over the entire land, embracing, it may be said, the four provinces.

The West at the present moment presents an extraordinary attraction of a higher kind to not alone natives in Ireland, but to all Catholics in these kingdoms as well as to their brethren on the continents of Europe and America.

The Catholic world has heard of the name and fame of Lourdes, once a wild spot but now frequented by all the world, far away in the mountainous region to the south of France.

A second Lourdes is arising at Knock, a small village surrounded by little hills, from which, as expressive of the natural character of the locality, it is known to the natives as the "village of the hills."

It is distant about six miles from Claremorris, which is favourably situated on the Great North Western Railway.

All this it is useful to state, for the sake of those who are now coming in numbers to visit at Knock, the scene of the apparition of the Blessed Virgin, and of St. Joseph and St. John which has been seen by the natives of that unpretending Nazareth.

The multitudes who, on today, Thursday, are flocking to the chapel, or Catholic church, at Knock from the surrounding districts are quite as numerous as those that form the monster meetings of the Land League which for some weeks are being held in the counties Mayo, Galway and Sligo.

As the people of the neighbouring towns, and of districts and counties more remote, aye, and the Catholics of England and America, take a great interest in the events that have lately transpired, and which at present are spoken of by everybody in this country Protestant as well as Catholic— relative to the supernatural apparition seen at the chapel of Knock, it is right to tell the public all the well authenticated facts regarding the multitudes and the miracles.

And first as to the multitudes. A vast gathering of people from all the border towns within a circuit of twenty miles are assembling on to-day, Thursday, at this unpretending little village.

Some of the pilgrim travellers start before day, guided by the light of the stars alone, and urged onward by the fervour of their own faith.

Some are seen wending their way on foot, others on horseback, while whole families of peasants proceed on their pilgrimage, journeying on the ordinary country vehicle known as a cart; the better class indulging in the luxury of sidecars or as they are known in Dublin by the name "outsiders"; not a few families from the different towns are cutting a dash by a tandem drive with the highest available vehicle in these parts, known by the unpretending and not agreeably sounding name of "drag"— a "handsome" would be quite a novel vehicle in this district.

The gathering here to-day is certainly enormous exhibiting at the same time, an agreeable diversity in the mixed character of the crowd assembled. The variety of individual character is co-extensive with the greatness of the numbers that compose the gathering.

Here, one can behold the blind, the lame, the crippled, the deformed, the deaf, the paralytic and epileptic—all seeking to be cured like those whom the Redeemer found at the Pool near Jerusalem.

Accounts without number are coming to our ears of cures effected here on the holy ground.

On this very day, in this blessed place, two remarkable miracles have just been performed on two persons who for years have, from the result of accidental causes, been unable to walk.

The man finds himself so greatly cured that he has left his crutches and is bounding home like the lame man cured before the golden gate of the temple of Jerusalem by St. Peter and St. John the Evangelist—walking and bounding along, and all the while giving thanks to God and blessing God's holy name.

Thursday and Monday are the days now set apart for visiting this place. This conclusion has been arrived at because the Blessed Mother of our Lord appeared on a Thursday and on Mondays not a few miracles are being performed on devotees who come to manifest their devotion for our Blessed Lady.

The fame of these miracles, and the story of the apparition too, are going abroad and creating an immense amount of conjecture and discussion amongst the people relative to the Natural and Supernatural world.

The children of the faith see nothing wonderful at all in these manifestations. They see nothing incongruous in the fact that they have occurred. The spiritual world is to them like a land with which they are familiar from the knowledge which their holy faith supplies, pretty much, as they are not put out of sorts with anything they hear or see from America— to them a far off land—because in this instance American life and habits are something with which they are familiar, for their relatives in that country commune with their friends in Ireland and tell them all regarding themselves and American life and manners in that great Republic to the West of the Atlantic.

In this way our Catholic people are no way put about by the narration of miracles or of miraculous apparitions at Knock.

They are by faith aware beforehand that such things happened before, happen now, and will take place as long as the church of God is on earth.

The angels appeared to Abraham, and walked with him, and talked to him and directed "him in all his ways." They appeared and spoke to, and brought to a foreign country and back, the son of Abraham, Isaac—the father of all the Israelites.

The same is true of Tobias and Daniel, the Prophets, and of St. Peter the head of the Apostles and of numerous saints in the Catholic Church in Africa, in Rome and in this and during the golden age of sanctity in Ireland.

What happened once why not happen again? It is the same God who ruled and governed mankind then as now; it is the same church that points out to her children the way, the truth, and the life.

The Irish faithful like those in the times of St. Columcille, or at an after period, are the brothers of the Redeemer, purchased by His sacred blood. He loves us as he loved them and sends his angels to take charge of us, as they took charge of them in days past.

OUR LADY OF KNOCK

Brighter than worlds of sunbursts beaming—
Fairer than myriad fair stars gleaming
Whiter than floods of moon waves streaming—
Lovlier far than the lovliest seeming—
Vision of love, of a pure heart's dreaming—
The blight of the night of lost life redeeming—
    Our Lady of Knock!
Thy beauty the heavens and earth transcending
Purer than crystalline dews descending—
On the lips of the virgin rose low bending—
Softer than rays of the rainbow blending
Tint into tint, in the heavens depending—
Sweeter than incense clouds ascending,
When the organ its silvery peal is lending
To the aid of the supplicant voice attending—
    Our Lady of Knock!
In the least of thy charms more wonders combining,
Than the mightiest mind in its art designing—
Fairer than milk white lilies entwining,
Their petals of gold round their heart's snow lining—
Cherubim, Seraphim, all outshining—
Far above mortals' or angels' divining—
    Our Lady of Knock!
"Queen of all queens", bespeaks thy brow—
Virgin of Virgins, we fervently vow
To thy service each day that our lives allow—
Life of our life! to thee we bow—
Hope of our hope we thee avow—
Joy of our joy! we hail thee now;
Love of our heart's deep love art thou—
    Our Lady of Knock!
Consoler of Erin! art thou not so?
Come in the night and the might of our woe_
In the storms that blast, and the winds that blow,
O'er our poor motherland drooping and low,
Forsaken of friend, derided by foe—
Thy mercy show, and relief bestow
On the hearts that break, and the eyes that flow
With tears—still the fears that their sad souls know—
    Our Lady of Knock!

MERVA
Published in "The Weekly News",
Saturday, February 14th, 1880.

Our Lady Of Knock,
Queen of Ireland.

CHAPTER 4
The Church of the Apparition

A correspondent who signs himself T. O'C, Limerick, comes to Knock via Claremorris in February, 1880, to see the church of the apparition, and to gain as much first-hand information as he can, for the newspaper to which he contributes.

The contents of this chapter are based upon the report which he writes for his newspaper, "The Limerick Reporter and Tipperary Vindicator" and which is published in the edition of Friday Evening, February 13th, 1880.

On arrival in Claremorris he meets the parish priest, Very Rev. Ulick J. Canon Bourke, a distinguished Gaelic scholar.

Canon Bourke decides that he will accompany T. O'C. to Knock so that he may facilitate the correspondent in any way he can.

The following is a description of the journey from the town of Claremorris to Knock church:

We leave for Knock at 3.30 p.m., having first paid fare on a one horse car—the fare no less than seven shillings and drivers' fees, a few shillings, for which John was thankful as a two shilling fee is rather rare thereabouts.

The road from Claremorris to Knock is remarkably bad—indeed Mac Adam seems never to have visited that quarter, and the county surveyor, whoever he is, ought to look to the bonds of the road jobbers.

The country around is desolation itself; here and there large patches of water cover the unreclaimed ground, and here and there, up and down, amid these hills and valleys, a silence prevails affording little or no proof of human energy or exertion.

We have a view of the celebrated Croagh-Patrick from the road to Knock..........

Near this is a gentleman's seat, hard by a stream in the valley and close by an ancient castle.

There are few houses on our way, and the state of the cabins in which the people dwell, is lamentable in the extreme.

The road within a few miles of Knock is in a most wretched state, cut up with cars, made mud of, and almost impassible to the thousands who make a pilgrimage to Knock, with hearts swayed by strong emotions, and in the earnestness and strength of sincere convictions.

We at length reach our destination at Knock, and recognise the Parish Church from what we have previously heard of it, though we are not prepared to see that it is really the handsome, well-proportioned building that it is.

Viewing it as we approach, its cruciform shape, and handsome square bell tower, with corners crocketted and pinnacled, and a cross rising from the apex of the roof, displays much good taste in its architectural features, not indeed to be expected in these remote Mayo hills. The tower is 60 feet high, and is furnished with a full toned sonorous bell which may be heard a great distance as it calls the people to Mass. The tower stands on the north end.

In the tower there is an aperture inside which opens into the church, and which forms a place for a vocal choir with which the services are supplied. The height of the church is 30 feet to the top of the gable, and about 24 feet wide; its length is almost 60 feet and the transverse section, which comprises the southern end, is 50 feet in length.

The gable is topped with a plain cross of large proportions. It was on the face of the gable wall that the apparition was seen on the 21st August.

The sacristy is situated immediately behind this wall.

At the time we enter the church, it is thronged.

The interior of the church is rather bare; small stations of the cross; no benches, except a few private pews; one confessional; and over the altar a not very well done painting of the Crucifixion.

The floor is of cement; but is now all cut up, and pitted into holes, the people carrying away the cement, which renders it impossible to keep one's foot upon it.

The altar is a plain one—the facade supported by two plain pillars at either side; and a stained-glass window above, which is inserted in the gable "Gloria in Excelsis Deo" is the legend over the altar.

A lamp always burns before the tabernacle in which the Blessed Sacrament is constantly preserved for the adoration of the faithful.

A wooden railing curves round in front of the altar steps.

The altar of the church has near it a small image of our Blessed Lady of Lourdes on a stand surrounded by lighted tapers of wax.

The tabernacle is made of wood, with a gilt carved glory around the top.

There are no ornaments, except a few vases filled with flowers, now rare in winter but the crocus peeps out and the mountain fern, and busy hands do the pious work of having the altar and all its surroundings clean and as neat and orderly as possible.

There are two stained-glass windows in the gables of the aisles; they indicate how anxious the parishioners have been to make the House of God worthy of a place for worshipping Him.

There is no ornamentation on the ceiling of the church, which is of plain white; no dust, no cobwebs, no proofs whatever that the caretaker does not do his duty.

The church is capable of containing a congregation of about six hundred persons; and thoroughly well-packed are the people as they pour in to hear Mass.

The Archdeacon gives out notices to the congregation and exhorts them in Irish—he speaks to them in English too; but they seem to love the old tongue, and the prayer for the dead in the Celtic is something to be heard and remembered: it is deep, solemn, touching the heart and penetrating to the inmost recesses of the soul.

There are two Masses on Sundays—one at 9 a.m., the second at 12 noon.

On every week day there is Mass at 9 a.m., except when the Archdeacon is at the stations.

The crowds have not room in the church, and they throng about the avenues, and into all accessible and into all almost-inaccessible places, and such is the position which they take that one finds it very hard to elbow his way into the church if he be not early.

The choir is rather scanty in voices; it consists of only two female voices, which are accompanied by a harmonium. I had the happiness of joining them in some selections during the celebration of Mass.

There is always Benediction of the Most Holy Sacrament after last Mass on the first Sunday of the month.

The male and female National Schools are within the enclosure of the church yard; and in the same churchyard there is a solitary cross in memory of Fr. Patrick O'Grady who had the church of the apparition constructed between the years 1828 and 1830.

The female children in the school, though poor, are neatly and cleanly attired, a point on which Miss Anderson, the intelligent teacher, insists, and which seems to be settled as a rule.

Around the sacred edifice is a low loosely piled stone wall, enclosing some flat grass grown land.

On every side except the western, which is bounded by a good road, the enclosure is joined by fields.

Inside the wall, somewhat to the east of the south side of the church, and about 25 or 30 yards distant, is the schoolhouse for the girls of the district and directly north of it is a similar type of schoolhouse for the boys.

On the southern side, the graveyard descends with a gentle declivity, and, again rising, stretches onward an undulating extent.

On the side of the road opposite to the church, and about a minute's walk from it, is the house of the parish priest, the Very Rev. Bartholomew A. Cavanagh.

After some little time I proceed to visit the scene of the apparition; and here I may say my feelings are more intensely agitated than I can describe.

Nothing however can surpass the inconvenience of the ground which is all a heap of mud, and which obliges me to secure a stone on which to kneel, as if I kneel in the mud I shall have it very hard to rise.

The evening is falling fast, a westerly breeze sweeps along and is somewhat cold.

Hundreds of pilgrims are on the spot, praying in a manner such as I have never before witnessed, praying abroad under the canopy of heaven, praying with an abated fervour, strong in faith, praying loudly, so as that the chorus of the united voices as they join in the Ave Maria in Irish or other prayers, constitute a strength of intonation such as no music can equal of organ or attuned note.

The scene reminds one of the description given by St. John Climachus in his "Holy ladder of perfection" of the deep abiding fervour of the penitents in the desert as they smite their breasts, and cry out for mercy, and beg of God the favour of grace, and beseech him to take into consideration their manifold imperfections.

Neither the thickening clouds which now come heaving up in the west, and bearing night closely on their track, nor the wind as it comes down among the hills and makes the air keener, nor the impassible condition of the ground beneath their feet, has the least effect in checking the extreme ardour of their devotion.

They pray aloud to the Blessed Virgin Mary, to the Infant Jesus, to the angels and the saints; they are there of all ranks and degrees, from all places, some with their vehicles.......

Archdeacon Cavanagh, the excellent pastor of Knock, is at this time in the sacristy hearing confessions, and the numbers who are coming to relieve their consciences of the burden of sin, are incalculable.

Before leaving the village, I go once more to visit the church. It is now a long time after dark. The thickness of the gloom renders it no easy task to make one's way. Around the lonely church the wind dismally moans and whistles.

Rain falls in drenching torrents from a scarcely visible sky.   Through the windows of the church there shines a light so faint that I doubt if it will be noticed except by an eye of keen inquiry.

The doors stand open, one and all. I enter and look around.

Motionless forms are to be seen on every side. Some are seated on rows of benches on either side of the altar, immediately outside the sanctuary railing. Others are kneeling in front of the altar. Others, apart, are almost prostrate, and little groups are praying together before the pictures of the stations of the Cross. A solemn hush pervades the dim interior.

I now see that the lights in the church at night-time are precisely such as have been stated to me by the Archdeacon—a dim red light from the sanctuary lamp; a faint white light from the lamp on the Virgin's altar; one candle within the sanctuary; and two or three others at points in the body of the church where one person is reading a rosary or a litany, whilst a group around him joins in the responses.

It may be said that these lamps and candles, faint and few, only make the darkness visible. The strip of wall above the altar is painted over, and by day it looks dark green, but now it appears as black as ink.

The lower portion of the Apparition gable after its covering of cement has been carried away by pilgrims.

MARY

Mary!
Sweet is your name!
Our mother's own from all eternity.
Rejoice,
Loved innocence of God,
Chosen from the beginning of the universe.
Your humble origin
Is no bar to heavenly favour.
Saint of Heaven?
Why not?

The little house,
The hungry fields,
The milking shed.
Treasure chests
In the garden of the Lord.

Tell us, Mary, what you see
Upon the way,
By yonder gable,
In the rain.

TOM NEARY

Heaven's radiance bright there shines,
Above the verdant meadow grass.
The Queen of Heaven,
St. Joseph,
St. John,
Guardian of her youth and
Protector in age.
The altar,
The Lamb,
The Cross.
Angels in the heavenly light.

Thrice blessed, Mary,
Child of grace,
Witness to Ireland 's Nazareth.

Little wonder then you run,
To tell your kinsfolk,
The good tidings of joy.
Their milking pales,
They throw upon the ground
And fly
To where the glory is.

Dear child of Knock!
Pray that we may one day know,
That glory which you see,
Upon your way,
One August evening
In the rain.

Byrnes' Cottage where five visionaries lived.

Mary Byrne, Visionary of Knock ,

A GRATEFUL HEART

A grateful heart This statue gave,
To Mary Queen of Knock.
Her way of saying she thanked her there,
On the spot where she had stood.

This Dublin maid no sight she had,
To enjoy creation's gifts,
Till there at Knock, in its cradle days,
she saw the light of day.
What gift from God and Mary dear
What a cure to thrill the heart?
"O Lord that I may see this day!"
She saw and gave her thanks.

With loving hands the artist worked,
to create this Madonna white,
in Portland Stone, with queenly gait,
as the Seers of Knock had told.
And when completed,
it was placed,
on the spot where she had stood.

Her Faith it was that made her whole,
from darkness into light.
May we be fired with a Faith as strong,
And may we also see!
And may we also see!

For the road of life is often dark,
and we are far from home;
the gush of Grace is what we need,
to light our narrow way.
This much with Faith
are treasures true—
All the riches we will need,
to gain salvation from the Lord,
in His dwelling fair on high.

So, with grateful hearts,
Let us give to Him,
To Mary Queen of Knock,
Our way of saying we thank her there,
on the spot where she has stood.

Tom Neary

Above: **Knock Church in 1879.**
Below Left: **the Apparition gable after the cement has been removed from the topmost part despite a covering of boards on the lower part.**
Below right: **An interior view of the Church in 1879.**

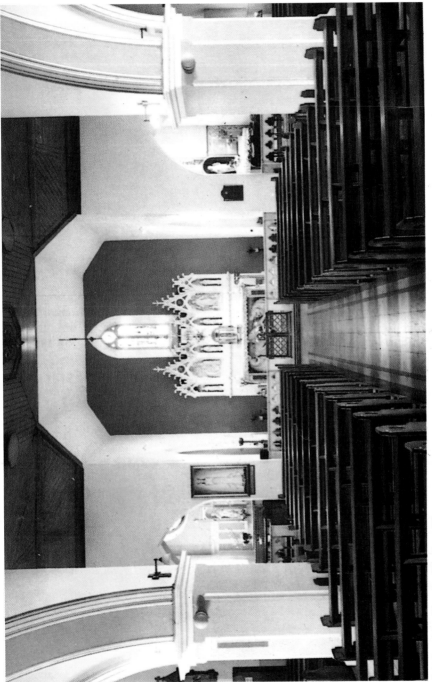

Interior of the Church of the Apparition.

CHAPTER 5

Interviews with the Visionaries

This chapter contains a number of interviews with the visionaries of Knock. They are based on the interviews which appear in the newspapers early in the year 1880.

Mary Byrne, Visionary of Knock, privileged daughter of the Mother of God,

The interviews with the members of the Byrne family and Mary McLoughlin are conducted by Mr. T.D. Sullivan of "The Weekly News" and they appear in the edition of Saturday, February 14th, 1880:

On presenting myself at the house of Mrs. Byrne which stands a couple of fields from the high road, and in the immediate neighbourhood of the church— I find the family occupied in extending hospitality to quite a number of visitors. Some are neighbours, who have happened to drop in for a chat on their homeward way from the village; others— travellers from a distance— are anxious, like myself, to hear from the lips of the eye—witnesses a full and particular account of the wonderful apparition of the 21st August.

Seated beside the kitchen fire, Margaret Byrne, the younger sister, converses with a group of women and girls, while Mrs. Byrne entertains the rest of the visitors in the parlour, and Mary, the eldest sister goes busily to and fro, providing some little refreshment for the guests.

As soon as Mary Byrne has discharged her household duties, she kindly offers to tell me of her experience of the 21st August, but I excuse myself for troubling her at a time when she is so busily engaged, and arrange to come back in the course of the day.

On my return, she ushers me at once into the parlour—a room betokening—not

Dominick Byrne, Visionary of Knock.

alone neatness but good taste—and after an offer of hospitality, made with a grace and cordiality often missing from the homes of wealth and rank, we proceed to deal with the object of my visit.

As I wait, I glance around, and see that the inside of the dwelling is comfortable and neat in its appearance.

The "dresser" familiar to all who visit Irish rural homesteads—stands laden with its rows of plates and dishes. The furniture of the apartment is suitably substantial, and various articles of home and farm use are carefully arranged about the place.There is no disorder visible; no trace of the want of a woman's hand. On the side of the kitchen next the entrance door there is another room, and on the side next the open fireplace a narrow passage leads, past the side wall of the chimney, to the parlour.

Before I report the interview, let me say a few words in description of Mary Byrne.

She is tall—very tall for a woman—erect in carriage, thin, black-haired, has an oval face with a tint of brown approaching almost to olive; regular features, and eyes, not very large, but dark and brilliant. She looks a questioner in the face when about to give an answer; her voice is agreeable; and she never delays to reply except when my question is such a one as calls for a special effort of memory.

I understand, Miss Byrne, I say, that you saw an extraordinary appearance here at the chapel of Knock.

Yes Sir, I did.

When did you see it?

On the 21st August.

At what hour?

About eight o'clock in the evening.

There was daylight at the time?

There was good light.

Where were you?

I was going from the house to the chapel.

Were you alone?

No; Mary McLoughlin, Fr. Cavanagh's housekeeper was with me.

Why were you going to the chapel at eight o'clock in the evening?

I was going to lock it up.

Well?

When we got to the wall by the schoolhouse, I looked up to the chapel and I saw the three statues.

Did the figures look like statues?

Yes; they looked so like statues, that I thought Fr. Cavanagh was after sending for them, and I wondered he never told us about them.

Apparition Chapel at night.

Apparition Chapel Exterior.

36.

What size were they?

About the same size as living people.

And what colour?

White.

Now describe the figure that appeared to be next the road.

St. Joseph was at that end of the gable. There was a stoop in him and he was facing towards the Blessed Virgin. I remarked his venerable grey hair and whiskers. His side face was turned to us.

What was the next figure?

The Blessed Virgin Mary. Her full face was turned out. Her two hands were raised up this way. (She holds up her own hands to show me how the hands of the Blessed Virgin were, in the Apparition). Her eyes were raised up in the form of praying.

Was every part of the figure the same colour as all the rest of it?

No; she wore a beautiful crown; it looked like gold; and the face appeared to be a yellower white than the body of the cloak.

How was the figure robed?

There was one large cloak, pinned to the neck, and falling loose over the arms, and there was another garment inside; it was tighter to the figure and there was something like "puffing" up the front of it.

Did you see the feet?

No; I couldn't see them; I think the robe covered them.

What was the third figure?

St. John. He was to the left of the Blessed Virgin. He appeared wearing a mitre and a long robe. He was partly turned away from the other figures, facing a plain altar, like marble, with a lamb on the altar, and a cross on the lamb's shoulder. There was a large book like a missal open on his left hand, and his right hand was raised up with the two fingers next us bent.

Did the figures appear to touch the ground?

No, they were about a foot off it; there was uncut meadow that time in the chapel yard; it was about a foot high, and the figures seemed to be just touching the top of it.

When you saw them first, did they seem to be up against the gable?

When we saw them first (that was from the wall of the schoolhouse) we thought they were a couple of feet out from the gable, and then when we went on, they seemed to go back into the gable, and when we came close up, they looked as if they were standing against the wall. I put out my hand, and thought to touch them, they looked so solid, and I found nothing. An old woman tried to kiss the Blessed Virgin's feet.

That evening was the weather wet or dry?

There was heavy rain coming up from the South against the gable, but no rain fell on the ground within two or three feet of the wall.

Was there any wind?

No.

How long did you stay looking at the figures?

From about eight o'clock until about half-past nine or a quarter to ten.

Was there any change in the appearance while you were looking at it'

It was just the same all the time.

Was it still there when you left?

It was.

Why did you leave?

We heard that a woman in the village, Mrs. Campbell, was just dying, and we all made off to see her.

Is she alive now?

No, she died a couple of weeks after.

The Apparition Scene, Thursday August 21st 1879

How soon did you go back to the gable of the church?

In about ten minutes. The place was quite dark then. The rain was pouring still.

Was the space about the gable still dry, as before?

No, it was wet when we went back.

How many people saw the appearance, to your knowledge?

I think there were about twelve.

Why were there so few people to see such a wonderful sight?

There would be a great many, but we were so rapt up in it, that we did not think of calling anyone.

Fr. Cavanagh's housekeeper forgot to call him out to see it. When she did tell him, at last, that she was after seeing the Blessed Virgin at the chapel, he thought that what she saw was the reflection of the stained-glass window of the Immaculate Conception. (this window was in the western transcept).

Did you ever see any strange appearance at the gable since?

No.

On the 21st August, as soon as you saw the figures, I believe you came back for your brother Dominick?

Yes; I ran back straight to the house.

Dominick was tired after mowing all day, and he was lying on the bed. I asked him to come out to see the Blessed Virgin. First he didn't give heed to me, but when I asked him the second time, and ran away out again, he ran out after me, up to the schoolhouse.

Did your mother and your sister Margaret come up at the same time?

No, they came a few minutes after. I sent down a little girl, Catherine Murray, for them and they came up with her.

Such is the story of Mary Byrne, as I have it from her own lips, in her own house.

The reader will observe that this account is fuller than any of the others, and enters into several novel particulars. The reason of this is simply that, as I find her prompt to answer, and anxious to clear up every point that seems to me to suggest examination, I avail myself in a special degree of her sympathy and intelligence.

Her manner during the interview is serious and collected; her self-possession is perfect; and, as I have before observed, she never delays to answer except when an inquiry is made which calls for an active effort of memory.

Margaret Byrne, the younger sister, is next called in.

She is wrapped in a heavy shawl, and appears to be in very delicate health. She is tall, like her elder sister, but otherwise there is slight resemblance between them; for whilst Mary is dark-eyed, brown-complexioned and quick of thought and speech, Margaret is very pale, with eyes of a bluish tint; she takes some time to reflect, and her manner of speech is slow, but this heaviness no doubt springs from the languor induced by long indisposition.

I ask her—Did you witness the apparition of the 21st of August?

I did.

How was your attention called to it?

My sister Mary sent Catherine Murray back to the house to call me. I went with her to the wall of the schoolhouse, where Mary and my brother Dominick, and Mary McLoughlin, the priest's housekeeper, were together.

The witness then goes on to describe the appearance on the gable, and the occurrences of the evening until the family return to their home.

In all that she says to me, her sister's evidence is confirmed. She relates nothing new.

The mother, Mrs. Byrne, next comes in. She is a woman well on in years, and must have been tall and stately in her youth. Now she is very much bent and wasted.

Her dress is that usually worn by the elder women in the country—white cap, crossed shawl, dark gown, and apron.

She impressed me as a person of considerable intelligence, and her readiness to answer was quite evident.

How did you come to know, Mrs. Byrne, I ask, of the appearance on the 21st August?

Catherine Murray, the little girl, came running into the house, and she said, "Come on till you see the Blessed Virgin at the chapel!"

What time was that?

I think it was eight o'clock, or a little after.

Did you go out at the same time as your daughter Margaret?

I did. We went up to the wall of the schoolhouse, where Mary and Dominick and Mary McLoughlin were before us.

Mrs. Byrne then gives an account which is practically a repetition of that already supplied above.

I ask to see the little girl, Catherine Murray, and she is brought in at once. She is not more than about nine years old.

I find her very shy and timid, but I gather from her that she also has seen the three figures on the gable as described, that she had been sent from the schoolhouse wall to call Mrs. Byrne and Maggie, and that she had gone back again with them.

While I talk to the little girl she keeps fast hold of Mary Byrne's dress, and when I ask her what size the figures on the gable were, she answers, an upward glance at her protectress, "They were as big as Mary!"

I shall now deal with the narrative of the young man Dominick Byrne. He acts as assistant to Archdeacon Cavanagh.

He is a tall, well-knit young fellow, erect and lively, with a small and shapely head, an aquiline nose, a keen dark eye, and clear-cut, handsome features.

The expression of his countenance is open and resolute.

He speaks with rapidity, and answers a question almost the very moment it is asked.

He is clothed when I see him, in grey frieze, and wears high leather leggings. Dominick lives with his family—composed of mother, brothers, and sisters—in the thatched cottage, looking like an ordinary small farmhouse, which stands about a couple of fields from the high road, close by the church, and is approached by a pathway running outside the schoolhouse wall, at the southern extremity of the church enclosure.

I may add that I estimate Dominick Byrne's age at two or three-and-twenty. The scene of my interview with him is inside an empty booth in the field beyond the schoolhouse wall.   It is stated, I said to him, that you saw the apparition of the 21st of August. Is that true?

It is.

How was your attention drawn to it?

I was at home in my own house. My sister Mary left the house to go and lock up the chapel.

Did she go out alone?

No, Mary McLoughlin, the priest's housekeeper was with her. Well, she wasn't gone out many minutes when she came running back into the house to me, and she said, "Come out now, if you want to see the Blessed Virgin!" "Yeh, where would I see the Blessed Virgin?" said 1. "Come out, come out," she said again, and I got up and ran out after her.

This happened in the evening?

Yes.

At what time of the evening?

It was going for eight o'clock.

Was there clear daylight then?

There was—bright day. I followed my sister until I got within a couple of hundred yards of the chapel. Then I saw the three figures outside the gable—the Blessed Virgin, St. Joseph and St. John. When I looked at them first they appeared to be some feet out from the gable, but I walked on to about four or five feet of them, and when I got as near as that, then they seemed to be up against the wall.

What was the height of the figures?

They were about life-size.

Did they appear to touch the ground?

No; they came down within about a foot of it.

Did the figures look flat, like pictures, or round and full like statues?

They looked like statues, round and full.

Now I wish you to describe them for me?

The Blessed Virgin was in the middle. Her face was turned out to us. Her eyes were lifted up, in the manner of praying. Her hands were this way. (The speaker places his hands so that the tips of the fingers are about on a level with the shoulders and the palms of the hands are turned outward.)

St. Joseph was on her right hand side, and turned towards her. His hands were joined together, and he was stooping. His hair and beard looked grey.

On the left hand side was St. Iohn. He was dressed in a long robe, and had on a mitre. He was turned partly out, and partly away from the Blessed Virgin facing an altar farther on to the left hand side of the gable. On his left hand he was holding a large book open. His right arm was lifted up in the form of blessing, and the fingers of the hand were this way. (The witness illustrates his evidence by holding up his own hand, with the fore and middle fingers stretched out, and the third and small fingers bent double, with the thumb placed against the joints of them next the tips.) The appearance before him was of a plain marble altar, with a lamb upon the altar, and a cross.

Were the figures, and all, of the one colour?

Yes.

What colour was that?

The colour of a bright whitish light.

Did the figures, or any part of them, or of the whole appearance, ever shake or waver while you were looking at them?

No.

Did the whole apparition seem to change position at all?

No; it did not.

Did you notice any flickering motion?

No.

How long did you stay about the gable?

About two hours.

Did the apparition go through any change in that time?

No; it remained exactly the same.

How many people saw it, to your knowledge?

About twelve or fourteen.

Tell me the names of some of them.

My mother, Mrs. Byrne, my sisters Mary and Maggie, a girl named

Catherine Murray, two boys, John Curry and Pat Hill, myself and another Dominick Byrne, and Miss McLoughlin, Fr. Cavanagh's housekeeper.

Did you see anyone touch the figures?

No, not one.

At what time did you come away?

About half past nine we all went away together to see a woman in the village that was thought to be at the point of death. When we went back, in about ten minutes to the gable of the chapel, all was dark.

And you never saw the figures, or any of them, again?

No.

This closes the evidence of Dominick Byrne respecting the appearance of the 21st of August.

His manner is free from anything like doubt or hesitation. He gives his answers readily and plainly.

I take my leave of the Byrne family with a decidedly strong impression in their favour. Everything I see of them—their appearance, their home, their manners—and everything I hear of them from neighbours who have known them all their lives, lead me to judge of them as honest, industrious and respectable people, whose word upon any matter to which they solemnly pledge it, ought to be treated with attention and respect.

My next interview is with Mary McLoughlin, Archdeacon Cavanagh's housekeeper, whose name has been so often mentioned during the course of this inquiry.

She is a person of middle age, robust and florid, with a loud voice, a steady flow of good spirits, and a very hearty and cordial style of address. I find there is no occasion to ask her any questions. She tells me what she has to tell without them.

On the 21st of August, she says—it was a Thursday evening—I wanted to go over to Mrs. Byrne's. (The two houses are scarcely ten minutes walk asunder.) About half-past seven o'clock I went in to Fr. Cavanagh (pointing to the sittingroom usually occupied by his reverence).

He was reading his Office at the time.I asked him for leave to go to Mrs. Byrne's.When he is reading his Office he never speaks to anyone, but he made a motion with his hand that gave me leave to go, and I went away at once.

I only stopped at Mrs. Byrne's a few minutes, and when I was coming out of it, Mary Byrne came with me to lock up the chapel.

Our way was up alongside the wall by the schoolhouse.

She then describes the apparition of the three figures and the altar on the southern gable.

I need not set down her words, nor do any more than state that they express the same experience as that of the other witnesses, whose evidence is already before you, readers.

Mary McLoughlin concludes—for a long time I didn't think of calling Fr. Cavanagh but when I came back I told him we were after seeing the Blessed Virgin at the chapel.

The interview which follows is based upon that which takes place between Patrick Hill, a teenager and visionary, and a correspondent of "The Limerick Reporter and Tipperary Vindicator".

This correspondent, who signs himself as T. O'C, Limerick, makes a point of meeting young Hill in the town of Claremorris before leaving for Knock with the parish priest of that town, namely, Very Rev. Ulick J. Canon Bourke. It is the good Canon who actually sends for Patrick so that he may be interviewed, as he lives in the town.

It is early in February, 1880, that the interview takes place and it is published in "The Limerick Reporter and Tipperary Vindicator", in the edition of Friday Evening, February 13th, 1880.

On arrival at Knock Shrine, His Holiness, Pope John Paul II acknowledges the welcome of the pilgrim thousands from the Basilica Ambulatory.

Mass in the Apparition Chapel

Interior of the Apparition Chapel

Patrick Hill is a frank, intelligent little boy of about 13 years. He answers the questions put to him readily and with animation. The following is the chief portion of the conversation which passes between him and me:—

Well, Pat, you live in Claremorris, don't you?

Yes, sir.

How came you to see the vision?

My aunt lives at Knock, sir, and I go there sometimes; on this night a man ran into my aunt's house and called us to come up to the chapel to see a miraculous sight that was there. The man's name was Dominick Byrne.

Then you went out; did anyone else go out with you?

Yes, sir, another man of the same name, Dominick Byrne, John Durkan, a servant boy, and a little boy named John Curry, about six years old.

Were there any persons there before you ?

Oh, yes, sir; there were people coming and going.

Well Pat, what did you see?

Here the little boy proceeds to describe the vision, giving substantially the account of it which the other witnesses have just given in their interviews.

He said he and the other persons who were with him saw a large space of soft white light on the gable of the church, the rest of the gable being quite dark at the time. In the midst of this light which was not exactly in the centre, but towards the left-hand side of the gable (as he stood facing it), he saw three figures; to his left, in a bending attitude, with hands clasped, was a figure of St. Joseph; in the middle a figure of the Virgin, her eyes raised, her hands raised to about the level of her shoulders and their palms turned outwards; to his (the witness's) right, a figure of a bishop, which the people said was St. John, holding in his left hand an open book, which he appeared to be reading, his right hand elevated, the thumb placed on the third and fourth fingers, the first and second standing erect. Farther on to his (the witness's) right appeared an altar with a lamb on it as represented in Catholic pictures, and a cross standing on the altar. All about the group were twinkling or flashing lights, like stars; they were not steady; they seemed as if they used to come nearer and then retire again, or to go in and out through the gable.

Was the night dark at the time, Pat?

Yes, sir, and it was raining very hard; we were all getting wet, but we didn't mind it.

Did there appear to be any light in the clouds overhead, or back of you anywhere?

No, sir, not a bit.

Where were you standing at this time?

Part of the time I and some of the others stood behind the low little wall that bounds the chapel field; we rested our elbows on it and looked at the visions, and the little boy that was with me (Curry) asked me to lift him up to see the beautiful things that were on the gable of the church. Part of the time we were in the field and quite near to the gable.

Did the figures appear quite distinct and round?

They did, sir.

Could you have touched them?

Yes, sir; and an old woman that was there tried to put her hands round the Virgin's feet.

Did you see the Virgin's feet?

Yes, sir, from the ankles down, she wore a white dress that reached to her ankles.

How high from the ground were the feet of the figures?

About a foot and a half.

How long did you remain there?

More than an hour. People were coming and going all the time. They all saw the vision.

What were you talking about while you were there?

About nothing only what we saw.

Did you say your prayers?

Oh, yes, sir: all the people went on their knees and were saying the Rosary and their prayers.

The Church of the Apparition in 1879 showing the Apparition gable and the Pilgrim Throngs .

Knock Basilica, Papal Cross and Apparition Chapel.

Knock Basilica showing Tapestry of the Apparition

48.

WELCOME TO ERIN'S SHORE

She has appeared; she loves our land:—
The land that Brigid loved, and Patrick trod:
Whose followers tread like them the ways of God,
Leading thousands upward in their virgin band;
Mirror of purity, robed in heaven's own sheen,
These are thy children—thou art their Queen!
We are thy supplicants! Welcome with thy store;
With succour, heavenly succour evermore.
Oh, gracious lady, kindly smile
On our ever-faithful Isle,
Strew thy blessings Erin's valleys o'er;
Queen of Heaven! evermore,
Thou art welcome to our shore.

She has appeared! She loves our land!
Sweet Virgin! Heaven's celestial Queen!
Bearing from God in her right hand
Blessings to Erin's Isle, I ween!
Erin! oppressed, despised; to Mary yet so dear
That she has come to thee, and lingers near
The humblest shrine within thy sea-girt shore:
Oh! bounteous Queen! welcome! welcome! evermore,
To Knock! to Erin! o'er and o'er!
Queen of Heaven! and as of yore,
Queen of Erin evermore!
Welcome to our shore!

Apparition Gable with the low stone wall in front and the female Schoolhouse on the right.

49.

She has appeared; she loves our land:—
The faithful land that Patrick loved and won
To Christ, the ever glorious Virgin's son!
She comes with blessings in her hand,
Ready to share the treasures of her queenly dower:
With Erin's children in their needful hour;
To prove our Island's faithful love
Endears us to her Son above.
Welcome, oh, Queen celestial! pour
The priceless blessings of thy store
On our Island evermore—Welcome to our shore!
She has appeared, she loves our land,
Whose saints in thousands mingle with its earth,
And tells by her extended hand
Of some great epoch 's fast approaching birth;
And great St. John, whose eagle eye hath scanned
The bright celestial domes—and Joseph, meek,
Have with the Virgin come to bless the land
That never yet grew faint nor weak
In faith, and hope, and earnest love
Towards Heaven's Lord and Queen above.
Oh, glorious Virgin, to whose sympathy revealed
No one ever yet once fruitlessly appealed,
Thou art welcome-aye, a thousand times and more
To Erin's poor, but hospitable shore—
To Erin's sainted hills—to unpretentious Knock!
To a poor peasantry, but a faithful flock;
Welcome with the richness of thy store.
The treasures of thy heart now pour
Upon our Island evermore;
Oh, gracious Queen, as when of yore
Our Erin rang from shore to shore
So let it be,
Now, in future and for evermore.
Isle of the West For ever blest!
By thy new guest,
Ring out thy joyous peals once more;
And sing thy welcome o 'er and o 'er.
Welcome to Erin's shore!

ANON. Newcastle West, Co. Tipperary. March 1st, 1880.
Published in "The Weekly News", Saturday, March 6th, 1880.

CHAPTER 6

`The Pastor of Mary's Poor

In this chapter we are introduced to the parish priest of Knock at the time of the Apparition.

All contained herein is based on the report of Mr. T.D. Sullivan of "TheWeekly News", which appears in the columns of that newspaper in the edition of February 14th, 1880:

The Archdeacon's residence stands about five minutes walk from the village and the church. It is not on the high road, but a few yards up a narrow by-way.

No pastor in the land occupies a more modest dwelling. The low thatched roof, the rude whitewashed walls, the few diminutive windows, all might lead the passer-by to look on it as the home of a small farmer, save for the low wall in front, the neat little wooden gate and the narrow strip of grass separating the dwelling from the road.

Here is the abode of a devoted ecclesiastic whose reputation for sanctity has spread far beyond the sphere of his ministrations.

The care of a large mountainous parish makes exacting demands on the energies of body as well as mind, and hence it is little time Archdeacon Cavanagh has to spare from the calls of his spiritual stewardship, but of the time he can call his own, the greater part is spent before the altar of that Church now linked with what may be perpetual fame.

I find the Archdeacon in his kitchen—the central apartment of his three-roomed dwelling—with its floor of clay, its open hearth and huge projecting chimney.

He is conversing with two or three of his brother clergy, and is surrounded

Very Rev. Archdeacon Bartholomew Cavanagh in front of his thatched cottage.

Eucharistic Blessing of the Sick at Knock.

Blessed Sacrament Chapel

Processional Statue of Our Lady of Knock.

by a little crowd of men and women of his flock, almost every one of whom have evidence to give of bodily ailments lessened or altogether got rid of by visits to the church of the Apparition.

The Archdeacon comes forward courteously to greet me. I am impressed, at the same moment, by the sweetness of his manner, and his commanding aspect. Though still in the prime of life, he is somewhat stooped, but so liberal is his stature that even with the stoop, he towers over men of average height, and has to look a good way down in conversing with the general run of people.

I must try in a few words to give an idea of his countenance and manner.

His forehead is lofty, his face long and full of healthy colour, his features regular and firm, his eyes blue, full and expressive; his whole air denoting gentleness and benevolence.

He speaks with an easy fluency; his manner in conversing upon interesting themes becomes thoroughly energetic, and he occasionally uses gesture with very telling effect to add to the expressiveness of his language.

I find him to be a most gentlemanlike, amiable and excellent clergyman, full of life and kindness; his fame is widespread all over Connaught, where rich and poor speak of him in the highest terms of praise—all things to all men, and goodness personified in all his relations with the country at large.

The Archdeacon is good looking, strong of constitution, between 50 and 60 years of age, energetic, active, cheerful, ever on the alert to meet every comer who wishes to see him.

His charity to the poor is unbounded—at one time he raffled his horse to raise funds to emigrate some poor girls who were in the workhouse.

He holds the distinguished position of Archdeacon of Tuam.

The whole work of Knock falls on the Archdeacon as the curate is attached to another chapel or church in the same parish.

What charms me most of all in him is his fatherly tenderness in speaking to his own poor people.

In the course of our interview, Archdeacon Cavanagh tells me of the eagerness of the people, who come in multitudes from far and near to possess themselves of fragments of cement or mortar from the wall of the southern gable.

When the cement that is near to hand has been entirely picked away, the mortar is rooted out from between the stones, and then the stones themselves are detached, and in a few days a large hole appears in the wall. A second hole is soon after made.

A sheathing of planks has to be put up, or else the wall will rapidly disappear. The Archdeacon goes on to speak of several cases in which persons undergoing some form of bodily suffering, who applied to the parts affected, water in which some of the cement had been dissolved, or had drunk water collected from the ground in front of the gable, were cured, or at least afforded much relief.

Referring to the apparition of the 21st August, he says: "When my housekeeper returned home that night, she said that she had seen the Blessed Virgin at the Chapel.

At first I gave no serious attention to her words, and afterwards when I began to think that a wonder may really have been witnessed, I concluded that the people did not leave the church until the apparition was visible no longer, so I remained at home that night.

Ever since, this has been to me a cause of the greatest mortification, but I console myself with the reflection that it was the will of God. It was the will of God that the vision should be shown to the people, not the priest. If I had seen it, and if, I had been the first to speak of it, many things, would have been said that cannot now be advanced with any fair show of reason or probability on their side."

Before I say good-bye to Archdeacon Cavanagh, he informs me that he has in his hands the depositions of fifteen persons, with reference to the visions at the church. They have been taken by a tribunal duly appointed for the purpose, and will be submitted in due course to the judgment of ecclesiastical authority. The reader is here reminded that the fifteen depositions are given in a special Appendix at the back of the book.

OH, MYSTERY ASTOUNDING!

Hail! most Blessed Mary, from God's high throne has come,
To sanctify old Ireland and heal the deaf and dumb.
To Knock's deserted chapel 'mid the mountains of the west,
Whose glory dims Mount Tabor and sets doubting minds at rest.

Oh, mystery astounding! Oh miracle sublime,
No tongue can tell the meaning nor heart of man divine,
Why Christ, the Eternal Wisdom, the just one and the true,
Should personate his Passion and all his wounds renew.

Poor, faithful, suffering Ireland, thy God has favoured thee,
More than all his vast creation, even the far-famed Galilee.
Oh, Joseph and Magdalene, and John the loved one, pray
That we be not unworthy on the last great final day.

ANON. Published in "The Cork Examiner", Saturday, May 22nd, 1880.

One of the Outdoor Stations of the Cross at Knock

The Sick at Knock in the shadows of the Cross

The Golden Rose presented to Knock Shrine by his Holiness, Pope John Paul II on the occasion of his historic pilgrimage.

CHAPTER 7
As a day in Galilee

A special correspondent of "The Weekly News" visits Knock and writes an account of his visit on the Monday evening of February 2nd, 1880.

His account is published in the edition of "The Weekly News" of Saturday, February 7th, 1880.

Another newspaper, "The Roscommon Journal and Western Reporter" carries the same account on the same date.

This chapter is partly based on the correspondent's account which deals mainly with cures, some of which he personally witnesses:

The period following the apparition is something similar to the period when Jesus walked the earth, working miracles.

At Knock the cry of the sick is no less constant than it was in His time. Any day of the week is as a day in Galilee: "Lord, have mercy on me a sinner"; "Lord, if you will you can make me clean"; "Lord, that I may see"; "Lord, that I may hear"; "Lord, that I may walk"; "Lord, he whom thou lovest is sick"; "Lord, say but the word and I shall be healed".

The response of the good Lord appears to me to be more than bounteous, for many are they that are being made clean, that are taking up their beds and walking, that are seeing, that are hearing, that are speaking, that are being healed, that are lame no more.

I meet, in the enclosure, Mr. P.J. Gordon, of Claremorris, his wife, and his daughter Delia, a pretty and most engaging child of twelve.

She is now the very picture of health and spirits.

Up to August she suffered intensely from attacks of violent pain in her left ear.

"Sometimes," says Mr. Gordon, "we had to get up in the night, to get flannel, hot whiskey, and different other remedies, to try and relieve her of the pain. This used to happen, perhaps, two or three times a week."

Mrs. Gordon then tells the story of the cure.

"On the Sunday next but one," she says, "after the apparition, I brought Delia here to Knock with me to Mass. While we were in the church the pain attacked her so violently that she began to cry. I brought her out to the gable, and bade her pray. I took the pin of my shawl, picked out a little of the cement, made the sign of the cross on it, and put it into her ear. At that moment a friend came up and spoke to me. She went away in a few minutes. I turned back and asked the child, 'Well, Delia, how is the pain?' She said,

"'Tis gone, mamma.' She never had a pain to trouble her since". Delia, lifting her timid eyes in reply to a question from me, confirmed her mother's account with a happy smile.

While I am talking to Miss Gordon, I hear a cry, "A miracle!" from the centre of the enclosure, below the gable.

Hastening thither, I find a poor man named Michael Nertney, a native of Tulsk, in the County Roscommon, relating that he has paid his first visit to Knock to-day, and that already he is partly restored to sight.

His eyes are nearly closed, and the lids very much inflamed.

How long were you blind?'l ask him.

Better than two years.

Were you able to see anything?

No, sir. If a match was struck close before my eyes I would just be able to tell there was some light—that's all.

I held my walking-stick about a yard before him.

Can you tell me what is this I have in my hand?

I can, sir; it's a walking-stick.

What colour is it?

Brown.

Is it smooth?

No; it has little lumps on it.

The answers were quite accurate.

If Michael Nertney, of Tulsk, was blind when he came to Knock this morning, he certainly is not blind when I see him and speak to him at three o'clock to-day.

Michael's cure is the ninety-fourth entry in Archdeacon Cavanagh's diary.

I conclude with brief notices of several marvellous cures, of some of which I have direct evidence, whilst others come under my personal observation.

On Saturday, a lady of property, Miss Burke, of Curraleigh, sister of Mr. Walter Burke, J.P., and Surgeon-Major Burke, of the Indian Army, is driven into Knock from her residence, a few miles distant, in her carriage. She has long been an invalid, and is as helpless as an infant for sometime past. She lies in her carriage recumbent, as if in bed. Four persons assist to carry her into the church—her mother, Archdeacon Cavanagh, her footman, and her maid.

She prays for a while before the altar; then, to the delight and

Invalids in Knock Basilica

The Apparition Church from The Calvary

KNOCK LOCATION PLAN

LEGEND

1. Apparition Chapel
2. Church of the Apparition
3. Stations of the Cross
4. Shrine Office & Information Centre
5. Audio Visual Prayer Guidance & Young Church Centre
6. Toilets
7. Mary's Garden
8. Papal Cross
9. Blessed Sacrament Chapel
10. Religious Books Centre
11. St. John's Rest and Care
12. North Bus and Car Park.
13. Basilica.
14. Family Life Centre.
15. Statue of St. Therese.
16. Msgr. Horan's Grave.
17. Legion of Mary Office.
18. Vocations Centre.
19. Our Lady's Domain
20. St. Joseph's Rest House.
21. Processional Square.
22. Holy Water Fonts.
23. New Chapel of Reconciliation.
24. Health Centre.
25. St. Brigid's Hostel.
26. Folk Museum.
27. ▷ To Carmelite Convent.
28. ▷ To Churchfield Presbytery
29. Caravan & Camping Park.
30. New Cemetery.
31. Old Cemetery - Witnesses Graves.
32. Calvary.
33. South Bus and Car Park
34. Statue of St. Michael.
35. Telephones.
36. Main Presbytery.
37. Main Shrine Office
38. Marriage Bureau.
39. St. Mary's Hostel.
40. St. Jarlath's Presbytery.
41. St. James's Presbytery.
42. St. Catherine Laboure Holiday Home.
43. West Bus and Car Park.
44. Souvenir Shops.
45. Post Office.
46. Garda Station.
47. Our Lady Queen of Peace, Nursing Home
48. ▷ To Kilkelly, Airport, Charlestown.
49. ▷ To Kiltimagh.
50. ▷ To Ballyhaunis, Dublin.
51. ▷ To Claremorris, Galway.

Photo: G. Bracken

Interior of the Apparition Chapel.

amazement of all observers, gets up and walks out of the church, and to her carriage, with no other assistance than that afforded her by her mother's arm.

To-day she drives up again to the church just as I happen to be standing by the gate.

I see her walk into the edifice, assisted by her mother, and, after an interval spent in prayer, I see her return with her mother to the carriage.

While moving about through the enclosure, my attention is attracted by a man named Thomas Killeen.

He cries out in a loud voice, "Praise and glory be to God! My sight is coming back to me!"

I make my way through the crowd that immediately surrounds him, and ask him what improvement he finds in his condition.

"Before I came to Knock," says he, "I hardly knew night from day".

"Now", he adds, turning round, so that he faces the sun, "I can see the sort of day it is, and I can see the people all around me. Praise and glory be to God!"

"Can you see," I ask, "whether this gentleman beside me has a beard?"

The man seems puzzled, raises his hand, and does not speak.

My friend holds up a gold ring between his finger and thumb, and questions "What is this?"

"'Tis something shining. 'Tis round. 'Tis like a ring."

The crowd cheer, full of sympathy and gladness, and Killeen continues to pray aloud, with every manifest sign of exultation.

Thomas Killeen is a native of Roslea, in the parish of Mayo and he has been almost stone blind for seventeen years.

The following pages contain extracts from the "Diary of Cures" kept by Archdeacon Cavanagh and that kept by Mr. John A. Gibney of Dublin.

All the extracts included here appear in various editions of "The Weekly News" commencing with the edition of Saturday, March 6th, 1880.

The extracts are presented by the special correspondent:

I now proceed to submit to you, readers, the substance of the diary kept by the parish priest of Knock.

He begins the record on the 31st October, 1879.

The date of the apparition was the 21st of August.

A cure of deafness and pain in the ear is reported ten days later, and several others in the course of the subsequent weeks, but Archdeacon Cavanagh takes no steps towards collecting and sifting the statements circulating amongst the people, until after the Archbishop of Tuam has appointed a commission to take evidence respecting the apparition, and after the commission has met, examined the several witnesses, and forwarded its report to the Archbishop.

By this time, the accounts of cures are numerous, indeed almost continual; the body of testimony increases from day to day; and the Archdeacon deems it his duty, now that the church, through his Grace of Tuam, has taken cognizance of the matter, to set down the exact particulars of such cures as can be proved to his satisfaction.

The diary opens with the words, "Ad Majorem Dei Gloriam" ("To the greater glory of God").

It is entitled, "An Account of the Miraculous Cures wrought at the gable of the chapel here, where the Blessed Virgin Mary, the Immaculate Mother, appeared, on the night of the 21st of August last."

A further note specifies that the cures have been wrought on persons who either prayed on the spot, or applied cement or clay taken from the church to the parts of the body affected by pains or wounds.

The following are the cases noted from the hundreds already recorded:—

Delia Gordon, daughter of Mr. P.J. Gordon, of Claremorris; deafness and pain in the left ear. This the first cure reported, was instantaneous. It occurred on Sunday, the 31st of August, 1879. The cure was effected by putting into the ear a small particle of cement.

Speech: Martin Bohane, County Tipperary, has recovered his speech; he has been deaf and dumb. He was partially paralysed in the right side and tongue. He is now quite well.

Palsy for 20 years: James Conglan of Tour, near Moate, County Westmeath. Cured this day, April 17th, of palsy. Badly for twenty years.

Epilepsy: Rose Herbert, William Street, North Strand, Dublin, cured of epilepsy.

Erysipelas: John McTigue, of Glasgow, has been cured of erysipelas he had in the face.

Instantaneous cure of Hip Disease: Hannah Pasley, of 9 Grafton Street, Dublin, was cured of hip disease. Was a very bad case. She is quite well. Instantaneously cured.

Speech: Michael Ryan of Templetuohy, Co. Tipperary, has recovered the use of his speech. He never attempted to speak previously.

Paralysis: Denis O'Conor, of Cahirciveen, Co. Kerry, cured of Paralysis.

Sight: Thomas McNamara, of Cloughjordan, recovered his sight at Knock.

View of Calvary with Basilica in Background.

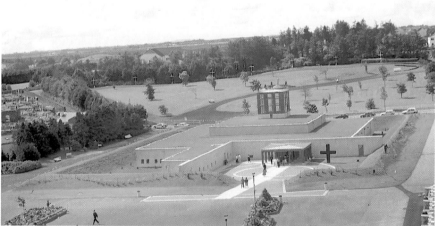

Chapel of Reconciliation

Hearing and Speech: William Hendrick of Enniscorthy, has recovered power of speech and hearing.

Cancer and Eye Trouble: Honoria Murphy, of Cork, is getting greatly improved in her sight and has been cured of cancer.

Dropsy: Bridget McGovern, Cloon, County Leitrim, was cured of dropsy and other internal diseases.

Heart Disease: Margaret Carolan has been cured of heart disease and general weakness of constitution and feebleness.

Paralysis: John McHinn, County Monaghan, was cured of paralysis.

Sight Returns: Mary Gallagher, Charlestown, County Mayo, blindness. After visiting Knock she was restored to sight.

Twenty-two years Deaf: On the same day the writer, and the witnesses with him, saw at Knock chapel a woman, aged about twenty-eight, who had been deaf since she was six years old, receive the power of hearing. The writer spoke to her, and she heard as well as anyone gifted with the faculty of hearing.

Ten years a Cripple: Mary Ryan, of Thurles, had been for ten years unable to go on her knees, or to move one inch without the help of a crutch. Her recovery enabled her to leave her crutch at Knock.

Paralysed for 20 years: Margaret Nee, of Moyrus. Paralysis. She had been in such an extreme degree deprived of the natural powers of motion that for twenty years she had been unable to go from one place to another except upon her hands and knees. Since her visit to Knock, her right leg has straightened. She is able to stretch it out and move it freely. The left leg is beginning to extend and become flexible.

Cancer: Michael Corcoran from Co. Meath. Cancer. His cure has been quite complete as a result of his pilgrimage here.

The following two cases are taken from the "Diary of Cures" compiled by Mr. John A. Gibney of Dublin who was instantaneously cured of Tubercular Hip in 1880.

Spinal Disease Instantaneously Cured (1880): Miss Jane O'Neill, an American lady of Irish birth, journeyed to Knock in 1880 seeking the favour of a cure.

She was suffering from serious spinal trouble and was carried to the church on a couch where she was placed before Our Lady's Altar. Except that her lips constantly moved in prayer she was as inanimate as a corpse.

For several days she remained at Knock and was carried to the church each day from her lodgings.

On the 8th September she was cured and her spinal plaster jacket with iron rod attached was hung on the apparition gable.

All those present at Knock saw her walking normally and without any trace of her terrible malady.

Instantaneous Cure of Spinal Injury: A lad was brought to Knock from England early in 1880 suffering from a serious injury to the spine received in a coal mine. He was carried into the grounds by his brother and another man and laid down before the gable of apparition.

He had barely touched the ground when he made a bound to his feet having been cured instantaneously.

The boy remained days and nights in the church breathing prayers and thanks.

The concluding part of our chapter is based on a report by the special correspondent of "The Weekly News". This report is published in the edition of Saturday, August 21st, 1880 and in "The Galway Vindicator and Connaught Advertiser" of the same date.

Only a small portion of this particular report is given here, namely, the portion which is appropriate to this chapter on cures:

But cures of bodily ailments are not for all. God does not so will these things. May it not be that a better thing is done for some of those humble and faithful pilgrims? May it not be that their spiritual wounds and bruises are healed, and their souls fitted for a place where there is neither sickness nor sorrow, and where they shall see in its fulness that glory the faintest ray of which they would so eagerly desire to behold for a moment in this world?

At all events we know that health is not to be gained by all who throng to any shrine, and that all truly devout Christians must be satisfied to submit to the will of God.

The quiet little burying-ground of Knock holds the mortal remains of some of the pious pilgrims who come from afar to pray in the church of the Apparition.   Over one of those new-made graves stands a wooden slab bearing the following inscription:—"Of your charity pray for the soul of Mary Ansbro, who died June the 2nd, 1880. Born at Oldham, England; aged 21 years."

Near this are two other graves of pilgrims, in which the interments took place on last Saturday and Sunday. One of these is unmarked by any inscription when I see it; over the other is a board on which the following words are scraped somewhat indistinctly:—"Martin Kenny; died August 12th, 1880. Of Boston; America."

Yes, of Boston, America, mayhap, of Clare or Limerick; back now from Boston to take his last rest in holy Ireland, the country of his fathers.

In the little church of Knock his fellow-travellers, men and women, come together and offer up prayers for his soul; there are Father Hogan, of St. John's Church, Trenton, New Jersey, Mr. Martin French, Mr. Hayes and others.

From the spot where the graves of Mary Ansbro and Martin Kenny are made, the gable of the church is full in view; from that spot the lights before the statue of the Virgin can be seen; to that spot comes the murmur of the litanies that are chanted on the hallowed ground.

Many an Irishman and woman far away over the wide world would think it

Pleasant to the grave to go
If one were sure to be buried so.

Cured pilgrims leave their sticks and crutches by the Apparition gable - evidence of the healing power of Knock.

FROM THE PILGRIM'S PEN

To tell my story, I would need, to write a thousand years,
And even then, I could not describe, the heartbreak and the tears,

That I, a drunken sot, had brought to dearest kith and kin,
Who saw me wallow in the mire, of drunkenness and sin.

The bar-room and the gambling house and those of ill-repute,
Were all that I frequented—now I was destitute.

The Mass, the Sacraments, the Church, had no place in my life,
And I had long since parted, from my once so loving wife.

And then, one night, I met a chap while walking by the dock,
Who talked me into going, on a pilgrimage to Knock.
I told him first "Now look you here....I'm not a holy Joe'
But after much persuasion, I did agree to go.

It was on a Sunday evening, I went into the ground,
And saw the thousands praying, as they walked the church around.

I laughed at them, those foolish folk, parading to and fro,
Expecting to see miracles, in this village in Mayo.

The invalids were taken out and placed before the shrine,
A young man on a stretcher, he had T.B.—the spine.

A young girl with cancer—yes, she looked kind of sad,
Only twenty-two she was—so young and yet so bad.

The wheelchairs, too, were pushed along and lined up at the altar,
While others walked with twisted limbs, their steps inclined to falter.

I waited then till Mass was read and each in turn was blessed,
And after all I'd heard of Knock, I thought, "well here's the test".

But I saw no-one leave his bed and no-one leave his chair,
Why boast of miracles to me, now what good all this prayer?

I looked again upon the scene, the blind, the maimed, the sore,
And yet each seemed to me to be, exactly as before.

I gazed upon each invalid, each handmaid and each steward,
And then I whispered, "Mary Help"—and I myself was cured.

A DUBLIN PILGRIM.

CHAPTER 8

Letters from all the World

To the Editor of "The Freeman's Journal".
Knock, Ballyhaunis, February 12th, 1880.

Sir,—I will feel obliged if you will make known to my numerous correspondents that it is simply impossible for me to answer the vast number of letters that arrive here daily from every part of Ireland, England and Scotland, relative to the apparition of our Blessed Immaculate Mother.

I take this opportunity of stating that the report given in the public journals are substantially correct, both as regards the apparition and the numerous miracles wrought here since the 21st of Last August,—I remain,

Yours faithfully,

Bartholomew Cavanagh, P.P.

The following is a very small sample of letters from the vast number received by Archdeacon Cavanagh and published in "The Weekly News" in 1880:

Church of the Sacred Heart,
Sharon, Mercer Co. Pa. U.S.A.,   **April 12th, 1880.**
Rev. and dear Father,

This morning was the last of the Novena made by the Sisters of the Humility of Mary for a young man named Jerry McCarthy. He is now about 18 years of age. He has had to use crutches from his infancy, as he was born reel-footed.   This morning himself and a large number of his friends went to Holy Communion! He then applied some of the cement from the chapel of Knock, which was given to him by Patrick McManus of this city.

The Blessed Virgin is as powerful at Knock as at Lourdes. Our Lord will not refuse any of her requests anywhere.

From this morning the young man laid aside his crutches and up to this time merely uses a slight cane, and walks erect and well.

K. O'Branigan, R.C.P.

Edinburgh,   **May 30th, 1880.**
To the Rev. Archdeacon Cavanagh.—

It is with a most grateful heart, full of fervent thanks to the Almighty

God, and with all possible praise and gratitude to His Blessed Mother, that I consider it my duty to report to your reverence the cure of my deafness in the right side of my head.

My entire right side was paralysed down to the sole of my foot; I was so troubled for three years. At my visit to the church at Knock, and on my second, I felt better and was cured on the 22nd of March, 1880.

I could not find it convenient to see you then in person, from the vast crowd of people, to inform you of the special favour which the Lord through His Blessed Mother had condescended to bless me with, and to beg your blessing and prayer, which I humbly beseech. I remain,
Yours most respectfully,
Margaret Sharky.

Sisters of Charity,
St. Joseph's Orphanage,
Hobart Town,
Tasmania.   **June 12th, 1880.**

Very Rev. Dear Fr.—The Sisters of Charity would feel most grateful if Archdeacon Cavanagh would send them some of the cement from Knock. They and all their poor people are most anxious to have some.

Every day almost, those who are afflicted express their ardent faith and hope that their dear Mother Mary will relieve them; they have the greatest confidence in her.

Already our dear Lady of Knock has shown her power in this distant land. A poor boy born blind has received his sight by applying some of the cement to his eyes.

The Sisters trust they are not giving you too much trouble, as they know you receive applications continually. They trust to your love for the poor "exiles from home."
Sisters of Charity,
Hobart Town, Tasmania.

Presentation Convent, Holy Trinity,
Sneem, Co. Kerry.   **July 27th, 1880.**

My Dear Archdeacon,—In May you had the goodness to send me a piece of cement from your holy little church, and it has brought blessings with it to our poor.

On Saturday, 4th inst., a woman came to the convent door, and on my inquiring her business she replied, "I want nothing, ma'am, but to give thanks!" and she threw herself on her knees and bent her head to the ground like the poor "stranger" in the Gospel "giving thanks." "For what have you to give thanks?" I asked. "For my sight," was the reply. "I came here for some of the 'blessed water', and since this day week I washed my eyes three times a day with it. I was so blind as to be almost entirely dark—I could scarcely find my way here to the door to ask 'the blessed water'; and now my eyes are all right, glory be to the great God and thanks to Him and you!"

I desired her to look up into my face, and I closely examined her eyes; they are indeed, to use her phraseology, "all right"— a fine, clear pair of good grey eyes, such as not to be looked for in a woman of her years. She was then after her confession, and was preparing for Holy Communion on the next or ninth day.   They call the "blessed water" that in which I put the cement you sent me. Many others have benefited by its use, but this woman is prominent in gratitude..........

Asking your blessings and prayers, your servant in J.C.,

M. de S. Carrick.

Belfast.   **August 3rd., 1880.**
Very Rev. Archdeacon Cavanagh, P.P.

Some months ago my attention was first called to the cure of Elizabeth Duffy, of Leeson Street, Belfast, aged sixteen—a pale, fair, anaemic girl, hardly able to walk, and suffering almost incessantly from pain.

On examination, I found a large lump in the groin, and three unhealthy openings in the outer side of the thigh. I expressed my opinion very strongly that nothing but a surgical examination, and, most likely, operation, could be of use. I gave her a little carbolic oil and morphia to allay pain. The morphia sickened her, as indeed I feared it would, owing to constitutional and stomach irritability.

I did not see Miss Duffy till nearly three weeks ago, on her return from Knock. The change in her condition was surprising. (I had seen the girl occasionally, but not as her doctor, on my professional visits to her mother's house, while attending a younger child; but declined to interfere unless the surgical examination were undergone.)

She had then become healthy and pleasing-looking, with red lips and full pulse and the "runnings" healed. I have seen her three or four times since, and each time her condition is better.

The lump in the groin is gone, and only the cicatrices of the three ulcers remain.

During the entire time she did not take a particle of medicine, the carbolic oil having been used only at first, and the morphia but a few times.

To-day I pronounce her well and fit for work.

I learn from her mother that the "running" had never ceased since she was a mere child.

To sum up, then, I believe that necrosis of the bone undoubtedly existed. I am confident that no medical treatment, change of air or good food could have brought about a cure so rapidly, or indeed at all; and I am forced to the conclusion, though sceptical about miracles, that the all-powerful interference of the Blessed Virgin has operated upon Elizabeth Duffy in a wondrous cure whilst at Knock.

John Campbell Quinn, M.D., L.A.

Greenock,
Scotland. **August 25th, 1880.**
Reverend Father,

I was suffering from rheumatic pains for the last thirteen or fourteen years. I was three times in the Greenock Infirmary, and I had to leave it uncured; but since my last visit to the holy shrine of Knock I have been perfectly cured, thank God! through the intercession of His Blessed Mother and the prayers of St. Joseph and St. John.

You will please remember me in your prayers.—I am,
Very Rev. Archdeacon Cavanagh, your faithful servant,
John McNicols.

Lancashire and Yorkshire Railway,
Dixon Fold Station. **August 31st, 1880.**
The Rev. Archdeacon Cavanagh.

Dear Rev. Father—On July 13th I had the happiness of receiving a little of the cement from you, which cured me.

For the last two or three years I was deaf in the right ear, and I am glad to say that the day after I tried the cement I could hear as well as if nothing had ever been wrong with me. I remain,
Your obedient child in Christ,
E. Graham.

The accounts of cures which follow have been sent to Ireland by an esteemed correspondent writing from St. John's Newfoundland, under the date, August 5th, 1880. All accounts appear in "The Weekly News" in September, 1880:

Margaret Doyle, of Gull Island, twenty-nine years of age, for the past eight years suffering from severe asthmatic fits, accompanied by acute pains all over the body and difficulty in breathing. Her life was despaired of and she received the last sacraments.

The attacks increased, till three years ago she became a confirmed invalid, scarcely able to move.

The parish priest, the Rev. Fr. Hanley, gave the poor sufferer a small quantity of water into which he had dropped a few particles of the cement from the chapel of Knock.

On the first application of the water, she exclaimed "I'm cured."

The following Sunday, and every Sunday since, she has been able to walk to Mass, a distance over half a mile. She has had no attack since and is growing stronger every day.

Patrick Hogan, of the same place, about eight years ago found his sight failing, so that after a year he could not well see to read. Objects became dim before him, "as if there were hairs over the eyes and thick, moving clouds."

Eventually he had to give up reading; boats on the harbour about seven or eight hundred yards distant appeared like black specks; and latterly he had become almost stupid from a severe and continuous pain in the head.

He procured some of the Knock water, applied it, and all but instantaneously the pain left his head.

Next morning, to his great joy, he found the film had left his eyes, and he could not only distinctly see the boats, but distinguish even the men aboard them.

During the time of his affliction, a lighthouse had been erected on Cape St. Francis across the bay, about forty miles distant. He had never seen it, but on the first night after using the water he saw the light for the first time.

Thomas McCann, of the same place, for twenty-two years a cripple (lameness caused by a chill). His right leg became so contracted that he could not put it to the ground; could not straighten or bend it; always felt a coldness in it; could not move a step without a crutch.

He went to the priest's house, received some of the water and applied it, and started for home.

On arriving at the chapel (about 100 yards) he felt a strange sensation, the coldness left the leg, and then and there he cast away his crutch and walked home with the greatest ease, a distance of about half a mile.

The crutch is now at the priest's house, and the most incredulous are forced to believe, as the man has been known to all as a helpless cripple for two-and-twenty years, and now walks about erect and firm as anyone in the place.

Joanna Collins, of Job's Cove, nine years old, had from infancy a pearl on her eye, which had given great trouble. Last Spring a violent pain set in, and the eye became very much inflamed.

The moment the water was applied, pain ceased; the pearl commenced to disappear notably on each application of the water. In three days it was gone altogether, and the child now sees with that eye as well as with the other.

Martin Colbert, of Job's Cove, aged twenty-three, born blind, one of the eye sockets is empty. In the other the white and pupil are about a quarter the size of an ordinary eye, much sunken and drawn towards the nose, so that any person seeing him would immediately pronounce him blind.

He craved to be brought to the priest's house, where he received some of the water.

The following is his statement:—Could never see any object. If a light were brought slowly across his eye he would have a dim perception of something being before him.

Applied the water at the priest's house, and on his way home received sight in the eye.

Could plainly discern the objects around him—such as trees and cattle,—and asked his uncle what they were.

He was especially astonished by sight of a waterfall.

Could see a person twenty yards off.

On first beholding the light he was in ecstasy, and exclaimed, "Oh, what a pretty thing it is!"

That same night he could see the moon and stars in the heavens.

When we saw him he had walked from his home unaided (his sister following him) to the priest's house, three miles, without being guided.

THE SUNLIGHT OF MARY'S SMILE

While famine stalked through the naked land,
While the people died, and the ruthless band
Of pitiless despots—and men still worse—
Who tempted the body the soul to curse—
Crushed the poor peasants by night and day,
Till the old and young in the churchyard lay—
For under the cross in its woe has been
For centuries seven our Island Green!

But the darkest hour to the dawn is nigh
To the glow of hope in the golden sky
Of faith and love, and the simple trust
Which guards as a relic our Irish dust;
For the shamrock lives o'er a saintly race,
And angels watch by their resting-place;
For the graves of the martyrs lie thick between
The verdant glades of our Island Green,

Mary of Knock, A heavenly ray of Hope.

Was it the power of archangels came
To Mary's people in Mary's name?
Or he the physician? or from the sky
Michael most like to the Lord on high ?
Was it Elias the prophet, sent
To our widowed land in her banishment?
Or Father Patrick? or Brigideen,
The virgins' pride in our Island Green!

As the mystic light of the gloaming fell,
With its tender glow, o'er the lonely dell,
'Mid the western highlands-far away
From the busy haunts of the proud and gay-
For the only science remembered there
Was the simple teaching of faith and prayer!—
To the sorrow-stricken, with mind serene,
Came the smile of God in our Island Green.

For the glory of God in the trinity
Of Purity, Patience and Love we see;
While the virtues we prized more than life or gain,
Bloomed bright in our land without blight or stain,
Came the "Lamb without spot"— for the lily 's bloom

Drew his heart by the spell of its sweet perfume!
Came Joseph and John and the Virgin Queen,
To bless and to succour our Island Green!

They came to bless, and they stayed to pray,
Within the week of Assumption Day;
When the Autumn winds blew chill and cold,
They came; and the incense and myrrh and gold
Of our grateful hearts made the angel choir
Shine forth in the gleaming of starry fire!
And the maimed and the sick found health, I ween,
When Mary smiled in our Island Green!

Oh, glory to God for the cross we bore!—
For the loved and the lost ones gone before!—
For the felon's cell and the convict's chains!—
For the myriad graves upon foreign plains!—
For the dead in the depth of the ocean wave!—
For our hearts' best blood shed in vain to save
Our race from a sorrow no land has seen,
Like the "Mary of Nations' our Island Green.

As snow, in the sunlight of Mary 's smile
Hath misery fled from our own dear isle!
Or if sorrows remain, 'tis the "chastening rod"—
"Badge of our tribe, " the elect of God !
Oh! Salve Regina! full well you knew
The tender love of our hearts for you.
For we welcomed the rack with its torments keen,
And we died for your sake in our Island Green.

As we bore the cross, so you brought the crown,
Dear Mother of God! in your sweet hands down—
Down from high heaven, so bright and fair,
To our people sore stricken with want and care!
For you knew that the sight of your radiant face
Would help us to suffer in faith and grace,
Till, crowned in the light of your love, dear Queen,
Through eternity's joy shines our Island Green!

Michael Davitt,
an earthly ray of hope

ANON
Published in "The Galway Vindicator and Connaught Advertiser",
Wednesday, May 26th, 1880.

CHAPTER 9

A Flame of Hope Kindleth

DAVITT ON THE MOVE

For some time now Michael Davitt has been travelling through his native County Mayo in order to obtain firsthand knowledge of the plight of poor tenants who are crushed by the burden of excessive rents.

Despite the failure of crops and the bad harvests, the landlords, far from reducing rents, have in some cases even increased them. Prospects are bleak indeed for 1879.

Davitt is convinced that some kind of organisation or League must be brought into being, in order to protect the helpless tenants and to oppose the power of the ruthless overlords, many of whom are pitiless.

A particularly bad situation has arisen in the Irishtown area of Co. Mayo. There, the landlord Walter Burke has doubled the rent, despite the bad conditions and the already big arrears of the tenants.

The matter has come to the ears of Davitt in Claremorris town and is determined to take the matter in hand.

A meeting is to be held in Irishtown on Sunday, April 20th, 1879, and the organiser is Patrick Nally of Balla, a prominent athlete. The Editor of "The Connaught Telegraph", Mr. James Daly, has promised to give publicity to the event.

THE IRISHTOWN MEETING

The Irishtown meeting, held to-day, has been a great success. Large numbers have been present from many parts of Co. Mayo and the estimated attendance has been put at 15,000.

A monster procession has come from the Knock—Claremorris area. Michael Davitt has not been present as he missed the train from Castlebar, but the resolutions which he had proposed have been passed.

Mr. Daly, in the course of the meeting has said that there have been 360 ejectment decrees obtained in Mayo alone, in a six month period.

This tenant demonstration in the village of Irishtown may well be the beginning of brighter days and happier times for blighted Ireland.

THE NATIONAL LAND LEAGUE OF MAYO.

At a special meeting, held in Daly's Hotel, Castlebar, Co. Mayo, on Saturday, August 16th, 1879, the National Land League of Mayo is founded by Michael Davitt.

In the edition of "The Connaught Telegraph", dated Saturday, August 23rd, 1879,the historic event is given full coverage.

The following extracts which are based upon that coverage, capture for the reader, something of that memorable day for the landless people of Ireland:

An influential and representative meeting of Tenant-farmers, merchants, and traders of Mayo has been held at Daly's Hotel, Castlebar, this day.

The following gentlemen have been among the large attendance: Messrs. John J . Louden, Westport; Michael Davitt, James Daly, and William Judge, Claremorris.

A statement has been issued, the more important aspects of which are given hereunder:

"The land of Ireland belongs to the people of Ireland, to be held and cultivated for the sustenance of those whom God decreed to be the inhabitants thereof. Land being created to supply the necessaries of existence, those who cultivate it to that end have a higher claim to its absolute possession than those who make it an article of barter to be used or disposed of for purposes of profit or pleasure...............

The landlord system which an alien government has imposed upon our country in the place of that which recognised no intermediate ownership between the cultivator of the soil and the State has reduced Ireland to a degree of poverty and social misery incompatible with the natural productiveness of its land and the progressive prosperity of other civilised nations.

The area of Ireland and the natural wealth of its soil is capable of supporting from twelve to twenty millions of inhabitants if restrictive land laws did not operate against the full development of the country's resources and the unfettered cultivation of the land; yet a population of eight millions previous to the year 1847 was reduced by death, starvation and exile, consequent upon an artificial famine and continued impoverishment, to little over five millions at the present day.

Decreased population, with its concomitant absorption of small holdings into large estates, has produced no beneficial change in the condition of the existent farming classes, who are compelled by the coercion of necessity, in the absence of manufacturing industry, to the acceptance of a non-alternative bargain, in the shape of exorbitant rent, in order to obtain the use of the soil.

The dread of eviction and rack-renting must necessarily operate against that expenditure of labour and enterprise in the cultivation of land and improvement of farm dwellings and premises which follow in every country where the fruits of the people's industry is protected by the State; hence the soil of Ireland is worse and less cultivated, and the living and habitations of its agricultural classes more wretched than in any country in the civilised world.

Over six million acres of Irish land is owned by less than 300 individuals, twelve of whom are in possession of 1,297,888 between them, while five millions of the Irish people own not a solitary acre.

For the protection of the proprietorial rights of the few thousand landlords in the country a standing army of semi-military police is maintained which the landless millions have to support, while the conduct of the landocracy in the exercise of its legal privileges occasions almost all the evils under which our people suffer..................

We appeal to the farmers of Ireland to be up and doing at once and organise themselves forthwith in order that their full strength may be put forth in behalf of themselves and their country in efforts to obtain what has brought security and comparative plenty to the farming classes of continental countries.."

The gloom and clouds appear to be clearing away and the God of day again asserts his sovereignty in the heavens. To-day, the glooms and troubles of ages are passing away from the Irish people, and the light of freedom, the rights of the people, are beginning to shine resplendently upon Ireland—a nation to be free and glorious once again.

The longest journey must come to an end, and a spirit is beginning to manifest itself among the people, which assures us that landlord domination has got its death-blow in Mayo.

A flame of hope kindleth and it shall not be extinguished.

THE IRISH NATIONAL LAND LEAGUE

An event which enjoys considerable publicity in the popular Press of Ireland in the late Autumn of 1879 is the founding of the Irish National Land League. The date of its foundation is Tuesday, October 21st, 1879 and its Chairman is Charles Stewart Parnell.

IRISHTOWN ANNIVERSARY

A reporter of "The Connaught Telegraph" visits Irishtown, Co. Mayo, on May 2nd, 1880. This is the date fixed for the celebration of the first anniversary of the tenant demonstration. His report appears in the columns of "The Connaught Telegraph", dated Saturday, May 8th, 1880.

The following paragraphs are based upon the above report and capture for us something of the occasion:

On Sunday a very large and enthusiastic demonstration is held in the now well-known village of Irishtown.

It is here some twelve months ago that the first Land meeting was held, and this demonstration has been organised to celebrate the anniversary.

In point of numbers and enthusiasm this meeting is as important as any previously held. Large contingents arrive from Westport, Balla, Knock, Ballindine, Logboy, Cross, Ballyhaunis, Claremorris, and Tuam. From all the surrounding districts the people pour in.

The Claremorris and Ballyhaunis brass bands are in attendance, and discourse national music during the proceedings.

Many banners bear the usual mottoes, such as "Ireland for the Irish",

Falling in for eviction duty, Ballinrobe district " *The Graphic"* London 1879.

"The Land for the people", "Is linn an Talamh", "Stick to your homesteads", etc. Messrs. Parnell, O'Kelly, Davitt, Daly and Louden are most enthusiastically received. A large force of police is present, and two Government reporters take short-hand notes on the platform.

At about 3 o'clock p.m., on the motion of Mr. Daniel O'Connor, Secretary, seconded by Mr. James Rhatigan, the chair is taken by the Rev. Fr. McAlpine, C.C.

Amongst those present are:—Messrs. Parnell, M.P.; J.J. O'Kelly, M.P.; Rev. James Corbett, C.C.; M.P. Boyton, Michael Davitt, J.J. Louden, James Daly, J.B. Walsh, Castlebar; J.W. Walsh, Balla; P.J. Gordon, Claremorris, Arthur O'Malley, Westport; H. Dalton, Dunmore, Hubert Monaghan, Ballinrobe; Richard Kelly, "Tuam Herald"; William Dorris, "Connaught Telegraph"; Thomas Sweeney, Andrew Grogan, J.W. Nally, Thomas McElinn, Thomas Costello, Tuam; James Bourke, do; Thomas A. Egan, do; Edward Caroll, do; George Pagett, do; P. Lyons, do; and John Healy, Glencorrib.

Mr. Michael Davitt comes forward amidst much enthusiasm and says—
"Rev. Chairman and men of Mayo, I take the liberty of moving the following resolution for your consideration:—

That in commemorating the initiation of the National Land agitation by an anniversary meeting in Irishtown, we are manifesting the vitality of that movement which during the past twelve months has shaken the feudalistic system of land laws to its foundation, called forth the inherent and hitherto inert resoluteness of the farmers of Ireland in the assertion of their rights, and demonstrated the power of the democracy of our country by the triumphs achieved over class supremacy, and the intelligence and order exhibited by the people in over one hundred great demonstrations during the past year.

Twelve months ago the cause of the tenant farmers was in the dust. To-day the cause of the farmers has triumphed, and although a famine has swept over the land, yet, thank God! the spirit abroad in Ireland is more national than it has been for the past fifty years.

The Land League calls upon the farmers to pay no rent until they get a substantial reduction. It calls upon the people, as I now call upon them, to look to their interests and the comforts of their homes first, and then give the landlord a rent that they can spare.

Now they have triumphed both over the Government of England and the landlords of Ireland, and by their action they have made the landlords the weaker party—then in the name of reason, justice, and common sense, let the landlords go to the wall".

CAPTAIN BOYCOTT

The news item below is based upon a report which appears in an edition of "The Ballinrobe Chronicle and Mayo Advertiser", dated Saturday, October 2nd, 1880:

It has just been learned that a method to be used by the Land Leaguers against the landlords is being called into play, for the first time, against an agent of Lord Erne, who resides at Lough Mask House, Co. Mayo. They promise to arouse considerable excitement in the area.

The agent's name is Captain Boycott and the local people there have decided upon a policy of non-co-operation in every respect.

THE CAPTAIN ONCE AGAIN

In an edition of "The Connaught Telegraph", dated November 6th, 1880, a correspondent gives a brief account of what transpires in the town of Ballinrobe, before his very eyes, on the previous Monday.

The paragraphs below are based upon the correspondent's account:

On to-day, Monday, Ballinrobe is made the scene of what at one time appears will end in a regular collision between the military and police on one side, the civilians on the other.

The cause of this riotous fray is, it transpires, that Captain Boycott— who has recently rendered himself notoriously obnoxious to the public— appears at Petty Sessions in three cases in which he gets defeated.

The gallant captain's appearance on the street although sheltered behind buckshot warriors, creates such wild fury and excitement that he and his bodyguard has to beat a precipitate retreat in the direction of the military barracks. Stones are used freely, Sub-Inspector McArdle, the R.M., and some of the R.I.C. coming in for what may be termed two-year-old paving stones. The "sojers" and police available have to turn out and guard this universally-held captain until they, by some difficulty, allow him to fly from his pursuers by the Castlebar road.

On the announcement being made publicly known that "the bird has flown" all things go as smooth as a marriage bell until it has been circulated that a volunteer brigade of Ulster Orangemen are expected to come to Lough Mask to save the harvest from the aspect of events. Doubtful if they do but they will find it enough to save themselves and not mind the harvest.

STRIKING SCENE IN CLAREMORRIS

The following piece of news from Claremorris is based upon a news item written in the town on Tuesday evening, March 30th, 1880, by a correspondent of "The Freeman's Journal". The news item appears in the columns of that newspaper and also in those of "The Weekly News", in the edition dated Saturday, April 3rd, 1880:

This morning great excitement prevails in the town and neighbourhood of Claremorris.

The two men, McHugh and Walshe, who last week gave possession of their houses to the Rev. James Corbett, C.C., start for America. Both have very large families, and the party numbers in all thirteen or fifteen individuals.

As early as six o'clock the Rev. Fr. Corbett, with some members of the Land League, arrive in the village of Ballintaffy, where the holdings referred to are situated. An immense crowd is assembling in the place.

Immediately on his arrival the Rev. Fr. Corbett gets a deep hole dug in front of McHugh's house, in which a stout young man places a long pole with a notice board on top, having in large letters the words, "Let no man take this land". The same is done opposite Walshe's house.

The Rev. Fr. Corbett next proceeds to put sub-tenants into the houses, whom he strictly cautions to keep "a firm grip"

RESISTING AN EVICTION IN CORK

The account of an eviction in Cork which follows is based upon a report of the incident in "The Irish Times", in August. 1880.

An edition of "The Weekly News", dated Saturday, August 28th, 1880, also carries news of the Cork eviction, but it takes the report from "The Irish Times":

The Sheriff, assisted by thirty policemen, proceed to-day to take possession of the farm of a man named Crowley, on the estate of J. O'Connor, J.P., near Dunmanway, Cork, Crowley having been evicted for non-payment of rent.

The farmhouse is barricaded and occupied by Crowley and several men arrive with pikes.

The Sheriff breaks in the doors under a heavy fire of stones and hot water, and the police, dashing in with fixed bayonets, overpower and capture the garrison, who are being brought to Dunmanway, and will be charged with forcibly resisting the legal process. There is great excitement in the district.

EVICTION NEAR LOUGHREA

The account given here of an eviction near Loughrea, Co. Galway, is based upon a report of the incident written by a correspondent of "The Irish Times", in Loughrea, on Friday night, September 10th, 1880. The report appears in that paper on the following day, namely, Saturday, September 11th, 1880:

This evening an eviction is taking place at Moreen, on Captain Dudley Persse's property, who resides at Roxborough, Loughrea.

Fearing a disturbance, there is a large force of police present, under the command of Sub-Inspector Carroll, of Gort.

There are some peasantry present, but there is no disturbance taking place. The evicted man's name is John Fallon, and he is a member of the Ballinderry branch of the Land League.

Later this evening the man and his family are to be removed to the Loughrea Workhouse, where, it is expected, they will remain.

THE LAND LEAGUE IN THE PROVINCES

In the edition of "The Weekly News", dated Saturday, June 26th, 1880, an account of the Land League in the Provinces is given in some detail.

The following extracts are based on this account with the exception of the one dealing with Headford, Co. Galway. The Headford item is based upon a notice which appears in "The Tuam News":

Meetings of every class and degree are being held through the country, in consideration of the widespread distress that now affects the small farmers and labouring classes in several parts of Ireland, and in the Western province to the greater degree and deeper and more sore-felt extent...... We have also had important meetings held in Dublin during the week, to a great extent in relation to the distress question, and to promote an improvement in the land laws of Ireland.

KILLEADEN

At a meeting of the Killeaden, Co. Mayo, branch of the Land League it is proposed by Mr. E. Lavin and seconded by Mr. M. Lavin:—

"That we do hereby pledge ourselves to maintain the principles of the Land League in all its suggestions, and to teach the people of our district their duty to themselves and their country—namely, not to take land from which tenants have been capriciously evicted, and to expose to the best of our ability all cases of landlord tyranny in our district; and also to organise meetings to protest against evictions; and never to relax our efforts until there is some measure adopted by Parliament to relieve our rack-rented countrymen from the distressing situation in which they are presently placed, by the grinding, extortionate system, landlordism".

Proposed by Mr. J. Reilly, and seconded by Mr. M. Grogan:—

"That every real tenant wrong brought to the knowledge of our local league, and coming within the sphere of its operations, will meet with cordial and prompt attention."

E. Lavin, Secretary.

LOUGHREA At Loughrea, Co. Galway, to-day, a placard is being issued calling upon the tenant farmers to "assemble in their thousands and show the tyrannical Chief Secretary and his Whig Government that they will no longer be deterred by threats."

FAIRYMOUNT A branch of the Land League has just been formed in the parish of Fairymount, Co. Roscommon.

The members are sending five pounds to the central council for the purposes of the League.

HEADFORD Placards are being posted to the effect that a monster meeting will be held at Headford, Co. Galway, on Sunday, for the purpose of establishing a branch of the National Land League in that district.

A deputation from the League will attend.

Delegates from other branches are also invited.

The placards conclude thus:—"Men of Galway and Mayo, assemble in your thousands and show to the world that you are determined to be no longer the serfs of a vile aristocracy. God save Ireland!"

LANDLORD MEETING

The account of a landlord meeting which is given hereunder is based on a report which appears in the edition of "The Weekly News", dated Saturday, October 16th, 1880.

This report is also published in "The Daily Express" and it is from this paper that "The Weekly News" takes the item of news hereunder:

A great meeting of landlords of Ireland, presided over by the Earl of Donoughmore, is being held in Dublin to discuss the state of the country.

It has been resolved to ask the Lord Lieutenant to receive a deputation from the meeting, and accordingly a very numerous deputation has been waiting upon His Excellency and Mr. Forster in the Privy Council Chamber of Dublin Castle, and has laid before them the conditions of the country and the urgent need of measures for the protection of life and property.

The Lord Lieutenant has expressed his sympathy, but has referred the deputation to Mr. Forster as being a Cabinet Minister.

Mr. Forster has assured the deputation that the Government have been doing and will do all they can within the law.

HAIL TO THEE, O QUEEN OF HEAVEN

Hark! the midnight bells are chiming,
Lo! the pilgrim host departs,
Bearing to the shrine of Mary
Grateful, loving, contrite hearts.

Chorus—
Hail to thee, O Queen of Heaven,
Hail to thee who bless'd our land
Limerick's sons here bring thee greetings
Bless our homes and pilgrim band.

Flashed the news o-'er land and ocean
Where the sons of Patrick roam,
Mary has again appeared
In their dear and Island home.

Chorus— Hail to thee, &c.
Near where Shannon 's foaming torrent
Courses past St. Mary's tower,
We have heard the gladsome story,
And depart at midnight's hour.

Chorus— Hall to thee, &c.
To thy shrine at Knock we wander,
Pilgrims of the night, to pay
Homage to the Queen of Heaven,
Mother bless us on our way.

Chorus— Hail to thee, &c.
Thou hast come in regal splendour
Joseph, John and angels near,
With the Lamb of God—our Saviour.
Pray for us and He will hear.

Chorus— Hail to thee, &c.
Spotless Lamb who died to save us,
Hear us through Thy Mother blessed,
Take away our sins and kindle
Love Divine within each breast.

Chorus— Hail to thee, &c.
Here where thou hast come from Heaven
Thou canst not refuse our prayer
May we ye return thy visit,
And in Heaven thy glory share.

Chorus—Hail to thee, &c.

Chorus on returning:

Midnight chimes again are pealing
Lo! the pilgrim host returns,
On each lip the name of Mary,
In each heart Divine love burns.

ANON.
The above hymn, sung to a grand old air, is the hymn of the Limerick pilgrims, to Our Lady of Knock, on the occasion of the first organised pilgrimage, in March 1880. they are members of the Archconfraternity of the Holy Family connected with the Redemptorists' church, Limerick. It is published in "The Limerick Reporter and Tipperary Vindicator", dated Tuesday Evening, June 29th, 1880.

Most Rev. Dr. John MacHale,
Archbishop of Tuam at the time of
the Apparition.

Very Rev. Ulick J. Canon Bourke,
P.P. Kilcolman, Claremorris,
Co. Mayo.
A distinguished academic and
ecclesiastic.
He was a member of the
Commission of inquiry. (1879)

Pope John Paul II moving through the Sick at the Basilica of Our Lady, Queen o f Ireland.

The scene in the Basilica of Our Lady Queen of Ireland at the beginning of the special Centenary Celebrations held on the feast of the Assumption, August 15th 1979.

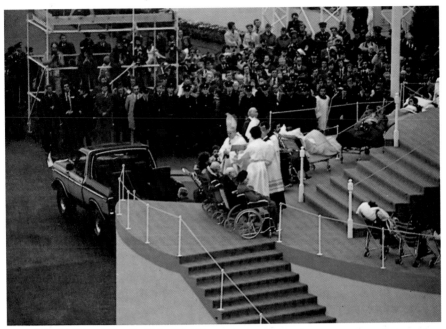

Pope John Paul II anointing the Sick at Knock.

His Holiness Pope John Paul II, celebrating Mass at the outdoor Sanctuary, Knock Shrine, on the 30th September1979

CHAPTER 10

The first organised Pilgrimage

Many pilgrims and lovers of Knock will undoubtedly enjoy this chapter for it contains a full and detailed account of the first organised pilgrimage to the shrine, in March, 1880.

The account given here is based on a correspondent's report which appears in "The Limerick Reporter and Tipperary Vindicator".

This report is also carried, in full, in an edition of "The Daily Express", dated Friday March 19th, 1880. under the headline, "The Mayo Miracles":

It will undoubtedly be of interest to many readers to learn that a "pilgrimage" to Knock has been organised in the city of Limerick.

As this is the first organised "pilgrimage" to the Mayo shrine, it is reported here in full.

Fifty-two members of the Archconfraternity of the Holy Family belonging to the section of "Our Lady Immaculate", proceed on Saturday morning, in accordance with a previous announcement, on a pilgrimage to Knock, the scene of the recent apparitions, which are already filling the whole world with wonder.

The members of the Archconfraternity of the Holy Family, with the full sanction and authority of their spiritual director, the Rev. Father Bergmans, C.S.S.R., resolve to visit Knock on a religious pilgrimage, to go forth to "the

A group of travellers going the Bianconi way, under God's canopy, in the West of Ireland.

holy mountain", not as hunters after curiosity, but in the strong faith and earnest confidence of Catholics solemnly impressed with the conviction that in the twinkling of an eye the Lord can do and undo, can give and take, can change the course of nature, and move the moon and stars at His will.

Impressed with these ideas the pilgrims, fifty-two in number assemble on Saturday morning at seven o'clock in the Church of St. Alphonsus, hear Mass, partake of the Bread of Life, and having returned to their respective homes to breakfast, meet at ten o'clock at the Limerick Terminus, and leave it by train amid the congratulations and blessings of large numbers who see them off en route by Ennis and on by the Athenry junction to Tuam.

One of the Archconfraternity goes before them to Tuam and Claremorris to make preparations for their reception, and have all matters essential to their comfort and convenience in travelling sufficiently well arranged.

We should state that the Prefect of the Section, Mr. James O'Meara, of Roche's-Street is the bearer of a grand banner of the Immaculate Heart of the Blessed Virgin Mary, work of a thoroughly gifted and accomplished hand, which was painted and prepared by him whose best sympathies are in

The Banner: On right of Altar

the good work, and to whose unceasing services the Archconfraternity is deeply indebted for its present noble position. We have no authority to mention his name, or to hint it; so on that point we are silent. He wants no human praise, though he merits all that can be said of him.

All goes on well on the way. The morning is balmy; the day is equally fine; and at three o'clock the ancient Archiepiscopal city of Tuam is reached, where the pilgrims at once proceed to the cathedral church of St. Jarlath, and make their visit to the Blessed Sacrament.

They are surprised with the beauty and majesty of the cathedral; and they are anxious, if they can, to catch a glimpse of "the Lion of the Fold of Judah", who presides there,the great John of Tuam, now in his ninety-first year; but they are forbidden to tarry, and besides it is impossible under the circumstances that they can now see the illustrious Archbishop.

At Tuam the pilgrims dine, and after dinner several "char à bancs" and jaunting cars are in readiness for them, and in these they drive through, certainly no very interesting country, to the country town of Claremorris, where it is resolved that they should sleep for the night, and where "ample room and verge enough" is had for each and all, whose visit attracted much attention on the part of the people, who, however, have already heard of the cause of their coming.

It is rather late, some time after ten o'clock p.m., when they reach Claremorris, and at so advanced an hour, after a long day's travelling by rail and road, and as there is nothing to be seen in the town, the pilgrims proceed to their several hotels, where having partaken of supper, they betake themselves to rest for the night, aware that they must be up betimes on the following (Sunday) morning, and be at Knock in time for first Mass, which is celebrated at 9 o'clock.

As our readers are aware, Knock is some six miles distant from Claremorris; the road is rough and hilly, but with joyous hearts, and good cars and charabancs, or long cars, and having slept well during the hours devoted to repose, the pilgrims are in time at Knock as the bell of the now celebrated chapel, the scene of the Apparitions, is summoning the congregation. Here the feelings of the pilgrims may be imagined; they cannot be described. Forming themselves processionally, headed by the Prefect (Mr. J. O'Meara), with the grand banner of Mary Immaculate unfurled—the bannerets borne by some of the pilgrims, and lighted lamp torches of varied colours by others, and chanting in strong and resonant voices from the Hymn Book of the Archconfraternity of the Holy Family, of which the Redemptorist Fathers possess the copyright, they move towards the chapel, where they are expected by the Venerable Archdeacon Cavanagh, the zealous parish priest of Knock. He warmly welcomes their arrival, and expresses his joy at meeting the faithful pilgrims of Limerick, as he calls them.

The congregation at Knock thus augmented by the accession of the fifty-two pilgrims from the City of the Violated Treaty, fills the chapel almost beyond its power of accommodation; but notwithstanding there is space sufficient for all.

The Venerable Archdeacon Cavanagh is the celebrant of Mass, unassisted by any other priest; the curate has to do duty in a distant chapel in the same parish. We need not say that "still they wonder, and still the wonder grows" among the Knockians, when they see the fifty-two pilgrims grouped around the altar rails, with banner, bannerets and lighted lamps, chanting a hymn in praise of Mary ever Virgin.

It is a sight which brought tears of joy and emotion to many eyes, and there are few who will not bear the memory of it green in their souls to the latest day of their lives.

The Venerable Archdeacon distributes Holy Communion to the 52 pilgrims; and at the conclusion of Divine Mass he addresses the congregation in a most effective, powerful, and persuasive address, in which he takes occasion to refer to the wants of the people of that district, and to the means that have been adopted to relieve them, and in which he speaks in the highest possible terms of praise of the pilgrims, who have come the long line of way from Limerick, who have heard the wonders for which Knock has become famous, and in the spirit of the ages of the Faith, have resolved to vindicate their principles by bowing before the shrine of the apparitions, and bearing witness to the multitude of cures that have been perfected on that spot. Sacred, he says, is that spot, for it was there that the Blessed Virgin Mary appeared, surrounded by angels.

After Mass the pilgrims proceed to the spacious schoolhouse, in the well-aired rooms of which.breakfast is prepared for them.

Last Mass is celebrated at 12 o'clock by Archdeacon Cavanagh, when the pilgrims in procession proceed to the chapel presenting a most affecting and impressive appearance. The procession goes round the chapel three times and having grouped around the gable, the scene of the apparition, the banner is temporarily placed on that portion of the gable on which it was stated the apparition of the Blessed Virgin was seen. The congregation is immense.

The procession then reforms, and passes into the church, where hymns of praise are sung, and the banner is placed near the Lady altar, where it is to remain in memory of the pilgrimage of the section of the Archconfraternity from Limerick. It should be stated that Archdeacon Cavanagh addresses the congregation in a most powerful and eloquent discourse, and imparts his blessing to the pilgrims and their families.

The pilgrims dine in the school-house at three o'clock p.m.

At five o'clock there is Benediction of the Blessed Sacrament, when the hymns are sung, and prayers for the intentions of the church and of each individual are recited.

At seven o'clock the pilgrims leave Knock amid the cheers and the blessings of the people, for Claremorris, where they remain that (Sunday) night.

Next morning, after breakfast, they leave Claremorris for Tuam, where they arrive about 2 o'clock p.m. On this occasion a deputation consisting of four of the pilgrims have the distinguished honour of an interview with the illustrious John of Tuam, now in the 91st year of his age, who receives them in his palace, speaks words of encouragement to them, blesses them and their families, and says in reference to the pilgrimage that it is a great blessing to the poor people of the West, in their wretchedness and misery and sufferings, that the Blessed Virgin Mother of God has appeared among them.

His Grace looks the personification of all that is noble, grand, venerable and illustrious. The pilgrims in a body visit the cathedral where they sing hymns and recite prayers before the Blessed Sacrament and recite the rosary of the Sacred Heart. They dine in Tuam, and leave the Archiepiscopal city for Limerick by train at 4 o'clock p.m. and arrive at the Limerick Terminus at ten o'clock, which they reach in pilgrim order, chanting hymns, which has been the case at each station on their way to the West, and home.

A large concourse of the Archconfraternity of the Holy Family receive them with cheers of welcome at the train.

We thus give a detailed account of the first pilgrimage to Knock.

SING, SING, MY SOUL!

Sing, Sing, my soul! our Christian hearts are swelling,
From north to south the news hath spread apace,
Through Erin's isle, lo! every tongue is telling
Of Mary's love for Patrick's faithful race.
Angels of Heaven! spirits unseen
Guard and protect us, the Pilgrims of your Queen.
'Tis Knock we seek, the spot of Mary's choosing;
On brothers, on, for Mary bids us come;
When She invites, our hearts know no refusing,
We'll praise Her there – in Her self-chosen home.
Angels of Heaven! &c.
Cheer up, old land! though want our hearts may sadden,
And dire distress makes felt its misery;
Mary has come! our troubled souls to gladden,
With uplift hands and eyes, She prays for thee.
Angels of Heaven! &c.
St. Joseph, too, in prayer, is bending lowly,
And John stands by, before the Lamb divine;
Mayo, rejoice! Heaven's Queen thy soil makes holy
and heals the sick who humbly seek Her shrine.
Angels of Heaven! &c.
Dear Angels bright! your faithful watches keeping,
Whisper sweet thoughts, brought fresh from realms above,
While on we speed, our senses lulled in sleeping,
Till Morn shall bring God's altar feast of love.
Angels of Heaven! &c.
'Twas Knock we sought. the spot of Mary's choosing,
Yes, brothers dear, She willed that we should come;
At Mary's voice our hearts knew no refusing;
Chant loud Her praise, in Her self-chosen home.
Angels of Heaven! &c.
We thank Thee, Lord, for this high favour given,
At Mary's feet our act of love to make;
When life is o'er, to see Our Queen in Heaven–
The boon we ask, O Lord, for Her dear sake.
Angels of Heaven! spirits unseen
Guard and protect us, the Pilgrims of your Queen.

Rev. Fr. Rooke.

Pope John Paul II in the Apparition Chapel.

A section of the well nigh half a million pilgrims who assembled at Knock Shrine for many hours to greet the Holy Father.

A Touch of 'Fashion 1880

CHAPTER 11

Lady Day in the Springtime

In the following pages, the reader can recapture the essential aspects of the feast of the Annunciation on March 25th, 1880.

That such a feast of Our Lady is marked by large crowds at Knock, is not surprising, as the Irish people, even in the worst of times, pay special homage to the Mother of God on the occasion of her feasts.

The contents of this chapter are based upon the report of a Special Correspondent of "The Irish Times" writing in the town of Ballyhaunis, Co. Mayo, on Tuesday, March 23rd, 1880, and published in the edition of that paper, dated Friday, March 26th, 1880.

Other newspapers to carry the report are "The Weekly News" of Saturday, April 3rd, 1880 and "The Galway Vindicator and Connaught Advertiser" of the same date:

For a few weeks past enormous crowds have daily visited the little chapel of Knock to practice special devotions there.

To-day being a festival of singular veneration in the Roman Catholic Church, the assemblage of people in its immensity of numbers far exceeds all previous gatherings. March 25th, 1880 will long be remembered.

On arriving shortly before one o'clock this morning at Ballyhaunis, which is about six miles distant from Knock, the change which its vicinity to that locality has effected is at once strikingly apparent.

Where once at nightfall the traditional quietude of a little country town reigned, there is stir and excitement.

Instead of the two or three passengers who heretofore travelled down by the night mail, several hundreds, nearly all of whom are sufferers in one phase or another of "the thousand ills that flesh is heir to" now pour forth from the compartments when the train arrives—the lame, the blind, the deaf, the deformed and the diseased.

The greater number of people proceed at once to Knock, and in a very few minutes every car available in the town is engaged to convey the people to the scene of their pilgrimage. Many who are so unfortunate as to be unable to afford a conveyance, or who cannot get one, walk the whole way, the strong assisting the weak.

And here I may observe that a rather conclusive sign of the prosperity that has so suddenly befallen the town is the fact that the outside cars have increased from five to nearly ten times that number.

A bianconi has also commenced running between the two towns, and Mr. Lyons, the proprietor of the hotel where I succeed in obtaining one of three beds stretched on the floor—so crowded is the house—is in treaty to run another of these "long cars", so vast is the traffic.

A flood of visitors like this cannot fail to materially benefit both Knock and towns like Claremorris and Ballyhaunis, situate near, but notwithstanding the great influx of visitors, no additional accommodation has been prepared.

I find, after having secured my bed, that no car can be obtained for, if not love or money, at least hire and seeking.

A small, open cart, jogging slowly along, drawn by a mule, proves the only vehicle.

Seated in this, my companion being a country girl, and Mr. Watson, who has already travelled forty miles in this fashion, I at length succeed in reaching the Mecca of my hopes.

All along the roads, parties of men, women, and children are met trudging on, and sometimes a group of wearied wayfarers are seen resting on the roadside.

The night is cold but fine, and the moonlight sheds over the tracts of bog and level fields, stretching on either side of the path, a bright silvery effulgence which renders every object distinctly visible.

As we draw near our destination the lighted windows of the chapel shine brightly over the landscape, and groups of pilgrims are more and more frequently met, till at length both sides of the path are lined with people, and cars and carts of all descriptions block our further progress.

All seem intent on hurrying forward, and none appear to regard fatigue. The architecture of the church is extremely plain, and indicative of economy in its every feature.

A weirdly strange and singular scene.

The enclosure and the ground outside are black with people of all ages, while within the yard turf fires, surrounded by a few bricks, are burning brightly. Crowds of women, young and old, are assembled around them boiling kettles of water for the making of tea.

Tents are erected and their interior is lighted with candles. In some, crowds of hungry people are partaking of some slight refreshment, and in others a brisk sale in rosaries, books of religious devotion, statues and pictures of the apparition is being conducted. All is business.

Contrasting with this busy scene of preparations are the silent worshippers, who kneel, wrapt in devotion, on the ground outside the brilliantly-lighted church; and turning from this to the southern end, the voices of a multitude engaged in prayer breaks on the ear with solemn impressiveness.

Inside, the church is densely crowded by a congregation, surging to and fro. Every available particle of room is occupied.

Here is enacted one of the most solemn and extraordinary scenes perhaps ever witnessed.......

The people begin to repeat aloud the "Ave Maria" standing. The crush is so great as to almost prevent movement of the arms.

Nothing is heard but the voices of people raised in prayer, while on the faces of young and old, men, women and children, are depicted enthusiasm and religious fervour in their highest degree.

They press towards the altar. Large crowds who stand at the three doors, having been unable to gain admission, crowd against the surging mass within...........

All night long these scenes continue.

Day at length breaks, and the light of dawn falls upon an assemblage of people whose fervour seems now as great as it had been when the clear cold moonlight shone through the windows of the church.

During the whole time I am in the chapel, and am so fortunate as to be a personal observer of what is taking place.

The morning is very cold, and after the atmosphere of the church its keeness is felt much more than it might otherwise be.

Breakfast is partaken of by the pilgrims and almost all present in the tents to which I have already referred.

As the morning grows later, contingents of people begin to pour in from Dublin and various other parts of the country, the numbers arriving enormously increasing as the forenoon advances.

As soon as the people reach Knock they either enter the church or kneel down outside praying with a devotion there is no mistaking.

Cars, carriages and carts draw up every minute, and contribute an additional socially better augmentation to the great assemblage present................

While some are kneeling in and outside the chapel, others are using sticks and stones on the cement and mortar of the south and south-east gable walls, which it is believed possess curative virtues, miraculous in their effect.

A portion of the wall has been boarded over to prevent it being carried away piecemeal, but this does not offer much difficulty to the people to-day, for a ladder having being scaled, the part above the boarding is attacked easily, and, to the recipients of the cement, satisfactorily.

A huge box near the church is filled with sticks, crutches and a wooden leg, left by those cured.

Large crowds continue coming and going the whole day long, so that judging from the enormous number, always present, the aggregate of visitors must be extremely great.

Shortly before 12 o'clock High Mass there cannot at the lowest calculation, be less than 15,000 persons present.

Some school children, who are about to receive their first Communion, attend dressed in white, with blue sashes and wearing on their heads white wreaths filled with roses..........

The place has become the centre of a pilgrimage of the most extensive nature. The fields adjoining the chapel are quite beaten hard by the feet of the multitude..............

The attendance to-day is the largest seen at the place.

The Apparition gable with a niche containing a statue of the Virgin on the left.Various apparate left by cured persons hang on the protective covering of boards. The man on the ladder is removing cement

AVE CHNOIC MHUIRE

A Bhanríon na h-Éireann!
  Céad fáilte go deo;
As ucht do chuairt chugainn,
  I gCnoc i Mhuigheo.
    Ave, Ave, Ave Maria.
    Ave, Ave, Ave Maria.
Tá drithle ag dealramh,
  Ar bharr do choróin;
Ag tabhairt sóláis dúinne,
  In aimsir an bhróin.
    Ave, Ave, Ave Maria
    Ave, Ave, Ave Maria.
Ar dheis leat, a Mhuire,
  Naomh Iósaf atá;
Is ar do chlé gléigeal,
  Ta Aspal an Ghrá.
    Ave, Ave, Ave Maria
    Ave, Ave, Ave Maria.
Faoi fhuinneoig na binne,
  Ta altóir an Uain;
Is cros ann mar chomhartha,
  Na h-íobairte buain.
    Ave, Ave, Ave Maria
    Ave, Ave, Ave Maria.
I shoilse na n-aingle,
  Gan fearthainn 'tá géar;
Tá muintir Chnoic Mhuire,
  Ag guí ar an bhféar.
    Ave, Ave, Ave Maria.
    Ave, Ave, Ave Maria.
A bhanríon! Ná tréig sinn,
  Tabhair cúnamh do chách;
Is beannaigh ar dtírne,
  Anois is go brách.
    Ave, Ave, Ave Maria.
    Ave, Ave, Ave Maria.

TOM NEARY

102.

CHAPTER 12
The Vigil and Feast of the Assumption

In "The Weekly News", dated Saturday, August 21st, 1880 is an account of the Vigil and Feast of the Assumption which take place on the 14th and 15th of that month, respectively.

The account is also carried in "The Galway Vindicator and Connaught Advertiser" of the same date.

What is written in the pages which follow is based upon this account:

That the Feast of the Assumption will be a great day of devotion at the Church of the Apparition at Knock is fully expected, and often thought of by many Irish Catholics since the commencement of the present month, not solely because that Feast of the Virgin is always highly honoured by our people, but also because it was within the octave—on the 21st August—the Apparition of Our Blessed Lady was witnessed at that favoured little church twelve months ago.

The managers of the Midland Railway, anticipating the strain that will be put upon their resources, make due preparations for the emergency, and organise a capital service of trains for the public convenience.

Rude and hasty preparations for the accommodation of the multitude are got up in the village of Knock, along the roadside, and in various other available places.

In the two nearest towns on the railway line—Ballyhaunis to the east, and Claremorris to the west—the hotel and lodging-house business receives an immense development.

Numbers of pilgrims who are unable to camp out in the open air or under the slight shelter of a tent leave those towns in the morning on vehicles of various sorts for Knock and return in the evening.

A comfortable hotel has recently been opened within a short distance—a mile at the utmost—of the Church of the Apparition, and is a great boon to all who are able to secure accommodation therein; but on such occasion as this it is, of course, inadequate to meet the public requirement, and great numbers of persons who are well content to pay for the use of even a chair or a sofa in any corner of the house have to turn from its doors to seek what shelter they can elsewhere.

Churchfield House as this hotel is called, was up to a few months ago the residence of a local Catholic gentleman, but to meet the exigencies of the present time it has been purchased or rented from him, and fitted up to suit the present purpose.

On Saturday, the 14th, great crowds begin to pour from all directions into the village, and most of them make almost immediately for the famous little church.

Of course, not a hundredth part of their number can get at any one time within its walls, but then they fill the spacious field by which it is surrounded, and fall at once to the practice of their devotions.

As might be expected, the space of gound in front of the gable on which the Apparition was seen is most densely crowded and passage through it is a work of difficulty.

I perceive that a scaffolding has been erected against the gable, which is to receive a new coating of cement.

The boarding on the lower part of the wall, which is all hung with crutches, will probably be taken away and a railing placed outside to protect the wall from further injury.

A rude wooden niche, or porch, in which is a statue of the Virgin surrounded by ornaments, candles, and flowers stands against the wall.

In the crowd which throngs the "chapel field" as it is called on Saturday evening, there are men and women from all parts of Ireland.

Many members of the Lancashire pilgrimage are there, and there also are some members of a party that have come from the United States.

Well dressed men, ladies in fashionable attire, children who have been tenderly nurtured and women in deep mourning for the loss of dear relatives are mingled there with peasants in homely garb and people in rags, with the lame, the halt and the blind..............

Some family groups lie on the grass, resting after their long and tiresome journeys; larger assemblages in other parts, kneeling, recite the Rosary.

Close by one of the boundary walls three little crowds, forming so many semicircles in front of three open umbrellas are to be seen. What is going on there? Approaching near to them, one finds the explanation: three priests are sitting on chairs holding those umbrellas over their heads, and hearing confessions—preparing penitents for Holy Communion next morning.

Then the candles in front of the statue of the Virgin, within the little niche are lighted and cast their rays on a dense mass of suppliants congregated in front. A murmur of prayer is over the whole field.

Turn where you will, now from one group and now from another, the Rosary and the Litany of the Virgin rise on the air.

So the hours wear on. Numbers of people now begin to "settle themselves" as well as they can for the night.

The countrywomen sit close by the walls of the church and of the field, pull their woollen shawls over their heads, so that each of them looks simply like a bundle of clothes, and in that position pray themselves to sleep.

And now up from the East, through the calm air of the Autumn night, smiling lovingly on the touching scene, comes the Lady Moon.

Still burn the lights before the statue of the Virgin; still rises the murmur of prayer on the air, till the sky grows white with the light of day, and the fair moon slowly disappears, and at half past four o'clock in the morning of the Feast of the Assumption the Masses begin to be offered inside the church.

All day long and all night the interior of the sacred edifice is crowded.

All day long and all night, prayers are going on there.

Some of the most delicate and helpless of the worshippers are placed inside the altar rails where they have a little space of boarded flooring beneath them, the greater number including several clergymen, ladies and gentlemen, and persons of all classes, sit out, or kneel out the time on the rough, earthen floor.

An immense number of communicants receive the Holy Sacrament at the altar rails, getting up to which is a matter of no small difficulty.

Later on in the morning Masses are said outside the gable in the open air, and I believe that never, not even in the Penal Times when "the wild rain dashed in the chalice, the priest's hands lifted up," is the Holy Sacrifice followed in all its parts with a more rapt and intense devotion.

Within the church High Mass is celebrated at 11 o'clock and the splendour and solemnity of the rite seems to still further exalt the feelings of the people who participate in it.

After the High Mass comes a procession in honour of our Blessed Lady, through the chapel grounds and around the walls of the sacred building. It is led by about a hundred young girls dressed in blue and white and bearing about a score of handsome banners, which have at various times been presented to the church of Knock by parties of pilgrims from Limerick, Cork, Manchester and other places. The girls are fine healthy children, and must have come from a wide circuit of the country, as the little village of Knock cannot turn out so large a contingent.

At the close of this interesting feature of the proceedings the Rev. Fr. O'Callaghan of Manchester mounts a temporary platform which has been improvised for him against the gable of the National School (which stands within the chapel field), and facing the Gable of the Apparition, he delivers an eloquent sermon on the Catholic doctrine regarding the Blessed Virgin and the glory and power of the Mother of God.

He dwells upon the reasonableness of that doctrine in all its parts, from the Immaculate Conception of the Virgin to her glorious Assumption into Heaven. He beseeches his hearers to have recourse to her as an intercessor with her Divine Son; he refers to the devotion towards her for which the faithful Irish race are distinguished; and he implores of them, from this place, hallowed by the vision she has given them, to maintain that glorious characteristic. He asks them to imitate the virtues of which Mary is so bright an example, and promises them that if they do so, they too will have, on the last day, a glorious assumption into heaven, there to live with Mary and Joseph, and with all the saints, with the Father, the Son, and the Holy Spirit, for all eternity.

At the close of the Reverend gentleman's impressive discourse the thousands who have attentively listened to it, and into whose hearts its every word appears to sink, throw themselves on their knees and pray fervently in accord with the appeal and with the spirit of the gifted preacher.

And when all these functions are over, still the devotions of the people go on, both inside the church and outside.

In the evening, there is Benediction of the Most Holy Sacrament, and when that is ended the prayers of the people still continue.

A considerable number of the devotees intend to remain on the spot until Saturday next, which will be the first anniversary of the apparition.

Pilgrim throngs in front of Knock Basilica

106.

CÉAD MÍLE FÁILTE

Bright angels are listening with rapture,
To murmurs of welcome so sweet,
From the grief-laden hearts of poor Erin,
Their own Mother Mary to greet!
From heath-covered hill-top and valley,
From every green leaf on the sod,
A céad míle fáilte is rising
To welcome the Mother of God!

To welcome the Balm of our sorrow;
The mother who watched thro' our woe,
And kept thy dear faith, martyr'd Erin,
As pure as thine own mountain snow!
Our guiding star upwards and onwards,
Whose blessed light hallows our sod,
Oh! céad míle fáilte for ever
To Mary, the Mother of God.

And céad míle fáilte, St. Joseph,
With the Master's beloved St. John,
Still near to the Empress of Heaven,
As in the dark days that are gone.
The great heart of Erin is throbbing,
And tears of love freshen her sod,
To welcome the favourites of Heaven,
Who came with the Mother of God !

Sweet Mother, stay with us for ever,
For much as we loved Thee before.
Since our isle has been blessed
with thy presence,
We love Thee a thousand times more!
And oh! when life's long dreary pathway,
Thy poor Irish children have trod,
May Thy céad míle fáilte, sweet Mother,
Then welcome us home to our God !

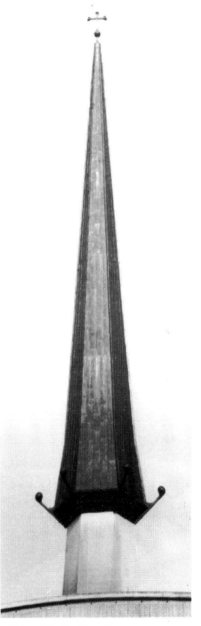

Spire of the Basilica of
Our Lady Queen of Ireland.

ANON.
The above appears in an edition of "The Cork
Examiner", dated Saturday Morning, June
26th,1880.

CHAPTER 13

A Candlelight Anniversary

Under the heading "Splendid Scenes of Faith and Devotion", the edition of "The Weekly News", dated Saturday, August 28th, 1880, gives a detailed account of the first anniversary of the Apparition at Knock, which is celebrated on Saturday, August 21st of that year.

The account of the first anniversary given below is based upon that which appears in "The Weekly News" referred to above:

A year having last Saturday elapsed since that August evening when the Apparition was seen at Knock, I revisit on that day the little, unadorned, but celebrated Chapel of the Mount, as in Gaelic the name of the locality signifies, as an interesting occasion upon which to observe the numerous changes that have been produced here by a vast influx of floating population.

Since my previous visit a surprising, and comparatively speaking, sudden transformation of the scene surrounding the church has taken place.

Where but recently a few distantly scattered cottages denoted the habitation of man, a town has almost sprung into existence.

Along the winding, hilly country road leading past the sacred edifice, and extending through bog, moorland and cultivated fields rich with a plenteous harvest, between Claremorris and Ballyhaunis, the two nearest towns, cars, cabs, waggonettes, carts and indeed every available means of conveyance are constantly seen filled with pilgrims hurrying to the shrine of their devotions, or returning homeward at nightfall, while humbler visitors at every rise and winding of the road, night, noon and morning are to be observed hastening forward on foot.

Men, women, and children, the young and the old, the healthy and the sick, form these pedestrian parties, all bent on the same common design, and as in groups they traverse the road, the strong assisting the weak, the old leaning upon the young, they impart a strange and animated, but melancholy aspect to the scene.

Deformity and disease are presented to view by many of these poor pilgrims, who, however, enlivened by that hope which "springs eternal in the human breast", often, despite their fatigue and sufferings, seem even quite cheerful as they near the destination of their journey.

Some wearied out by the long distance traversed, linger along the wayside to take a brief rest, or lean against the hedges and sit on the side of the ditches. These are soon joined by others, and then they pass the time in mutual condolence and encouragement till once more all set forward, for not a moment is ever needlessly lost, so intense is the desire and eager the longing to reach the end of the pilgrimage.

But, besides those, others are occasionally beheld who, without friends, and with, perhaps, scarcely a penny to maintain them at Knock, crawl along the wayside, unable to walk, presenting in their poverty and deformity a melancholy spectacle.

These, setting forth with a fatalistic reliance upon the future, and so confident of recovery could they but once reach the far-famed chapel, as, indeed, to be ready and willing to suffer any hardship, have travelled from distant country towns and subsist on the charity of the inhabitants of the places through which they pass on their long and toilsome journey.

Even, however, among the poorest, and the most wretched, kindliness and commiseration appear to prevail. Cheering greetings and salutations are interchanged, for unity in a common purpose excites mutual sympathy.

Of the vehicles, the poorest class consists of small open carts drawn by donkeys. and these conveyances frequently contain the most pitiable victims of the "thousand ills that flesh is heir to".

The occupants lie on straw, and as the cart lumbers slowly along they are constantly jolted at every inequality of ground crossed.

Nor is the pilgrimage confined to the poor, or the people of Ireland. The rich, and strangers from various parts of the United Kingdom and America, also perform it, and help to swell the never ceasing tide of visitors.

In addition, however, to the pilgrims who seek Knock from a belief in its miraculous cures, there are many, who, availing themselves of the cheap excursion trains visit the church from curiosity merely.

As the town—for it now almost deserves the appellation—is approached, the groups of pedestrians gradually become larger and more frequent, and the vehicles more numerous, until the roadway is for a considerable distance quite thronged.

Among the crowds seen at this portion of the journey are numerous little girls wearing wreaths of roses and tulle veils and plain white dresses, with a broad blue sash round the waist—the costume, by contrast with the bright colours so generally worn by country women, presenting a conspicuously pretty, light, and picturesque appearance.

And now one commences to see that full swing of business activity that forms so interesting a feature of a visit to Knock, and attests the enormous concourse of people that within the past year have travelled hither; and by their presence have so quickly caused the growth of this hugh encampment at a distance of not more than six miles from either of two towns.

On both sides of the roadway long lines of stalls and wooden booths, with sloping, canvas-covered roofs extend.

Before the open doors are exposed the most miscellaneous collection of provisions conceivable, and all placed together in curious juxtaposition. Bacon, apples, herrings, sweets, lemonade, potatoes, flour, eggs, tobacco, bread, biscuits, cakes and numerous other articles are seen, while within the tents similar stores are observable.

Nearly every shop or booth or tent, or with whatever name the erection may be dignified, contains the same kind of goods as its rivals, and the apparent object of each proprietor has been to fill his place cramfull with everything which experience has proved saleable at Knock, no matter how small the quantity, or how limited the dimensions of the tent.

The cooking is all done on the road, and in the most primitive manner. About three or four feet in front of each tent is a circular wall of large stones, about two feet in height, a foot or two in diameter, and open at the top. In the space so enclosed a turf fire is lighted and the culinary operations performed in the open air according to the sweet will and leisure of the cook.

All these stone enclosures are as nearly as possible in the same line, so that they do not interfere with the traffic, although occasionally the road is so narrow that when two cars are passing much anxiety must sometimes be occasioned the expectant diner.

In other tents, principally on the church side of the road, tea, coffee and cooked refreshments are provided for hungry and thirsty pilgrims, and, judging from the appearance of the gipsy-like restaurants, the service of the entertainment must be of a rather rude and primitive character.

On this occasion I did not test it, but on my former visit I breakfasted in one of the two or three tents which at that time were the only ones, and my experience then was more amusing in the recollection than agreeable in the incidence.

My seat was a basket turned upside down, my saucer was tin, but the cup, or rather a small bowl was certainly delf. There was no butter and no knife.

The bread was cut by a man standing at the foot of the long, dirty, uncovered deal table who placed the loaf between his knees, severed it into two junks, one of which he gave me, and the other he "conferred" upon rny vis-a-vis, for no other word would convey an idea of the emphatic solemnity with which he handed the piece.

However, since then things have doubtless much improved for now Knock has a hotel, and, besides the "shops", the refreshment tents are numerous.

On every hand during my present visit a brisk trade is being done, and the great amount of food consumed is indicated by the barrels of flour and fish, the sacks of meal, and the layers of bacon piled upon one another, which are exposed for sale. One flour "store" which I observed will perhaps afford some idea of the simple, yet ingenious manner in which commerce is carried on in this portion of the world.

It consists of a cart tilted up. From the shafts is hung a pair of scales, and a little to one side is a barrel of flour, the diminished contents of which bears satisfactory testimony of the success of the couple who are the owners.

Besides the above-mentioned means of obtaining refreshments, there are numerous stands and donkey carts stationed along the roadside, and filled with green fruit and cakes and other edibles of a dubiously tempting appearance. Some of the owners of these stalls sit contentedly on the boards amidst their wares, and form a curious feature of the extraordinary scene presented by the whole place, with its noise and commotion, and singular contrasts of brisk commercial activity and high religious excitement.

One thing however, it should be stated, cannot be purchased here and that is intoxicating drink, the sale of which I hear is forbidden by the Very Rev. Archdeacon Cavanagh, the parish priest of the district.

Before proceeding to describe the interior of the enclosure surrounding the church, it may perhaps be not uninteresting to mention as an indication of the prosperity which the apparitions have brought to Knock and the surrounding neighbourhood that a hotel has also been built about three quarters of a mile from the site of the church, and forty cars now are on hire at Knock, where twelve months ago a cart could scarcely be obtained.

In Claremorris and Ballyhaunis, the rival towns for the patronage of pilgrims, the cars and bianconis have been increased to more than double their original number, and are kept day and night busily employed, so immense is the influx of visitors. The hotels are also full, and in Ballyhaunis two new houses of entertainment have been established, while both in that town and Claremorris, and all along the way to Knock, nearly every cottage, no matter how small, affords accommodation to several pilgrims.

So thoroughly do the people rely upon the support derived from the travellers that every thought, idea, and plan seems based on the pilgrimage.

Reverting, however, to the church itself, since my previous visit the stone wall that encircles the sacred edifice, and which had been partially thrown down by the crowds that assembled night and day, has been rebuilt to its original height, and surmounted by a substantial coping of white stone, and now stands about three feet higher than when I last saw it.

Along the whole inner side of the western wall extends a row of booths in which are sold rosaries and crucifixes, pictures and statuettes representing some of the visions which are said to have been seen, ornamental penholders, crosses, lockets, and other little mementos containing microscopic views of the church and the apparitions and also a large number of photographs of the Rev. Fr. Cavanagh.

Most of the vendors in these tents belong to Dublin, but have come to Knock to take advantage of the golden harvest which is being reaped.

On my former visit the sale of provisions and the cooking of food over large turf fires were being carried on in the chapel yard, but to-day I find all that changed. Now no stalls are allowed within the gates save those for the sale of rosaries, pictures and ornaments—a wise and commendable regulation.

In strong contrast with the scene within the booths and without the walls are the audible, earnest prayers and rapt expression of the thousands of pilgrims standing, walking and kneeling round the church. On every side the deepest religious fervour seems to prevail. Everyone present is devoutly praying, and, as I walk through the ground, I pass scarcely an individual or group whose lips are not moving in loud or at half audible prayer. The devotional earnestness is intense and as 7 o'clock passes, and 8 o'clock draws near, it appears to increase, for many seem of opinion that this being the anniversary of the time at which the visions are said to have been beheld, there might be a repetition of the apparitions.

The greatest enthusiasm, however, appears to be among those who stand and kneel at the south-western side of the gable wall, before a niche in which is placed an image, artistically executed, in accordance with the appearance of the visions stated to have been seen.

Amid bouquets placed at the foot of the statue is the legend, "Our Lady of Knock".....

Besides the huge wicker-work receptacle, almost completely filled with sticks and crutches, left by pilgrims, as representing the cures miraculously effected, there are now three rows of similar offerings ranged in parallel and horizontal lines across the woodwork with which the lower two-thirds of the gable has been boarded over, so as to prevent the wall being totally destroyed by the pilgrims, in their anxiety to obtain a piece of cement or brick. Indeed, high above the top of the boarding the wall has been quite denuded of its covering, and it has been found necessary that it should be newly plastered over. Some of the fresh coating has already been put on.

A large inscription has been placed by the Very Rev. Archdeacon upon the wall, stating that the clay beneath is quite as efficacious as the cement, and the result has been that the ground has for several yards been taken up and removed, and the wall nearly undermined.

A large box bearing the words "Our Lady of Knock", is fastened to the woodwork of the wall for votive offerings.

Inside the church is unchanged from when I saw it on my former visit, except that now two new silken banners hang at the sides of the altar, bearing the figures of the vision and inscribed "Our Lady of Knock".

Boxes similar to the one outside are placed in the interior for the contributions of the congregation.

About 8 o'clock in the evening it is decided that a candle-light

The Candlelight procession in Our Lady's Domain.

procession will take place round the church and in a few minutes nearly four thousand men, women and children are marshalled in processional order, the lines being seven deep.

Each pilgrim carries a lighted candle.The procession is headed by a cross bearer, and acolytes and two large banners.

As the long succession of lines move forward the voices rising and falling as they join in song, and the whole place illuminated by the light of the candles, the scene is extremely impressive.

The women, who nearly all walk together, first commence to sing the hymn composed by the Rev. Fr. Faber, the well-known English convert to Catholicism, and as their voices die away in the distance the chaunt of a litany rises from the ranks of the men, to be succeeded in turn by the softer voices of girls singing "Immaculate, immaculate".

Round and round the procession moves about a dozen times, its van and rear meeting and forming one vast circle. As it advances, many who at first have remained sitting on the wall or reclining on the ground rise and join its ranks till a very inconsiderable number, comparatively speaking, are mere observers.

The group collected in front of the niche, however, still remain in their position.

At half past ten o'clock the procession ceases, and once more the air is filled with the voices of the people collected in circles, praying aloud, while one of the number recites a litany.

The chapel remains open all night, and is densely crowded till morning. The scene almost equals that which I have witnessed on my former visit; but upon this occasion the devotions of the pilgrims are directed by a priest from Manchester, instead of the lady who formerly undertook this duty.

The keeping open of the church till morning is granted by special permission, as for some time past, owing to the removal by pilgrims of portions of the wall at the side of the altar, a regulation has been in force by which admission to the sacred edifice is not allowed after ten o'clock at night, except to a few persons who are able to obtain the favour by personal application to the Archdeacon.

Yesterday an even larger number of people were present, and, as might naturally be supposed, the church was densely thronged throughout the day.

The stalls and booths were open as on the previous day, and the weather being warm and extremely fine, the scene was full of animation.

ON YOUR NATAL DAY

*We give you
the flowers,
That bloom fair in our land,
O Mary, mother of love,
On your natal day.*

*We give you
The candles,
That flicker in the autumn breeze,
O Mary, mother of joy,
And bless your day.*

*We give you
The prayers,
That fall from our lips,
O Mary, mother of peace,
And praise your day.*

*We give you
the songs,
That rise from your gable shrine,
O Mary, mother of Knock,
And cheer your day.*

*We give you
The loves,
That burn in our hearts,
O Mary, mother of silence,
And light your day.*

*You give us
The gifts,
That no money can buy,
O Mary, mother of grace,
On your natal day.*

TOM NEARY

The Apparition Gable with protective iron railing and statue of the Blessed Virgin of Knock

CHAPTER 14
A Happy Birthday

A pilgrim from Massachusetts, U.S.A., is present in Knock on the eve of the Feast of Our Lady's Nativity and also on the actual feast, namely, Wednesday, September 8th, 1880.

On the following Saturday, the pilgrim writes, at Knock, an account of what has taken place at the shrine on both days. When written, the account is sent to the Editor of "The Cork Examiner".

The account is published in the columns of that newspaper, dated Saturday morning, September 25th, 1880, and it is upon this that the chapter which follows is based:

Although the harvest season, always late in this part of the country, is now at its height, still it must be recorded to the praise of the people of the Knock district, that large numbers of them have left the world's interests behind them on the 8th September and are hastening here to Knock to honour the natal day of the Queen of Heaven, in the autumn weather of 1880.

All through the day on Tuesday, and all through the night there is a comparatively slow but steady influx of visitors to the shrine of Our Lady of Knock.

Three or four priests hear confessions on Tuesday evening and far into the night, thus giving all the pilgrims the much-desired opportunity of approaching the sacraments of Penance and the Blessed Eucharist.

On Tuesday night, at about half-past eight o'clock, a candlelight procession of about four thousand pilgrims makes a circuit of the church about five or six times. The procession is headed by a single banner, after which comes the pilgrim choir, composed of about twenty male and fifty female voices singing the Litany of Our Lady of Loretto and a number of sacred hymns selected for the occasion.

When this splendid act of devotion has lasted for about an hour and a half the choir stands in front of the holy gable, inside the large ring made around them by the processionists and give a fitting close to the performance by singing "Look Down, O Mother Mary", "Ave Maris Stella", and "Tis Heaven is the Prize". The number which then departs to spend the night in the lodging house is very inconsiderable—the best majority remain up all night reciting the Rosary at intervals of half an hour until morning.

On Wednesday morning, the Feast of the Nativity of the Blessed Virgin, the number of visitors here is at the lowest estimate eight thousand.

Masses are celebrated on both altars in quick succession, from half-past five in the morning until half-past eleven. Half-past eight o'clock Mass is celebrated by the Most Rev. B. Amherst of Northampton, England.

At 6 p.m. this distinguished visitor, assisted by Rev. John Kearney, (Father Cavanagh's zealous curate), gives Benediction of the Most Holy Sacrament. Frequently during the day the curate (the Venerable Archdeacon being absent, to the regret of many, on account of the serious illness of a near and dear relative), standing inside the altar rails, blesses the water, medals, scapulars, beads and crosses which the pilgrims carry away with them, as well for souvenirs of Our Lady of Knock as for devotional purposes.

The public and private devotions of the pilgrims during the day are, like those of the preceding night, fervent and edifying in a most eminent degree.

In this vast concourse of people busied with their devotions, each person prays to God, to the Blessed Virgin, and to the saints with as complete oblivion of his or her surroundings as if he or she is the only person in the world.

A notable and praiseworthy feature of the devotions here is how completely dead the people always are during time of prayer to everything else save the Celestial Being whom they are addressing. Human respect and a perception of inconveniences and discomforts are unknown at such times.

At about seven o'clock in the evening commences the crowning and most prominent feature of the day's devotion. The performance of the preceding evening is repeated on a much more extended and improved plan.

The Rev. Fr. Faunt of the diocese of Louisville, Kentucky, who, during his visit here, for the improvement of his shattered health, has proved himself an untiring servant of Our Lady of Knock, is kind enough, during the day, to select a programme and has copies of it distributed through the members of the choir, and to take active steps towards the formation and management of the procession.

A Cross-bearer, holding the richly-gilt processional Cross, which has been presented to the "Church of the Apparitions" by a gentleman from London, heads the procession.

Immediately after him comes four young men, bearing upon their shoulders a handsomely executed platform, holding a medium sized statue of Our Lady of Knock.

Around the statue is a small arch, clothed with nicely arranged natural and artificial flowers.

An abundance of the same attractive ornaments are scattered in artistic profusion around its base.

In front of the statue, upon the platform, are three lighted candles, with two behind it—emblematic, perhaps, of the Five Glorious Mysteries.

Immediately after the statue, the face of which is turned towards the people, come the children of Mary of the parish, robed in pure white and blue sashes, and handsome wreathes of flowers upon the veils which cover their heads. They walk four deep, and carry three beautiful banners.

Then comes the pilgrim choir, composed of about fifty male and two hundred female voices.

After the choir the vast body of the people file into rank, about ten deep.

At intervals of about thirty yards, through the large circle which this vast number of pilgrims makes around this hallowed little church, is carried one or another of the magnificent banners which have been presented to Our Lady of Knock.

As the procession commences to move, the choir begins to sing the Litany of Our Lady of Loretto. Every person in the vast assemblage, who has the least pretensions to being a singer, helps to swell the chorus of this magnificent prayer to the Blessed Virgin.

By the time the procession has gone once around the chapel the ranks are fully and orderly formed.

It is but just to state here, that Bryan Byrne, eldest son of the favoured Byrne family, renders no inconsiderable service in forming and preserving the ranks. About ten rounds are made of the sacred edifice, the procession, or rather the choir, for the procession reaches all the building, halting at the completion of each round in front of the holy gable, while a hymn or the Litany is being sung.

At the end of the tenth round, the choir, as they did the previous night, come together inside the starry ring of processionists, and give a grand and solemn close to the evening's proceedings by their splendid singing of "Heaven is the Prize", Sweet Sacrament" and the "Magnificat". What a happy birthday! During the procession, which lasts about two hours and a half, there are about a dozen clergymen upon the grounds, amongst whom is the Most Rev. Bishop Amherst. It is truly edifying to note the devotion of the people, and especially, if I may particularize, of the poor people during this glorious act of devotion to the Mother of God.

The lame, the infirm, the rheumatic, the blind, forget for the first time the impediments to locomotion arising from their deformity, their weakness, their pains, their inability on other occasions to take a single step in any given direction, and move around with the procession as cheerfully as though they are disinherited from all the "ills that flesh is heir to".

Poor people who find it hard enough to get a few pence to give in exchange for an humble supper, are still rich enough to invest three or four pence in a candle to light in honour of the Mother Mary.

To tell them that they can give sufficient honour to the Mother of God by fervent prayer without spending the little harvests gleaned from the charity of their brethren is of no avail.

Even though they are in rags, they will prove themselves loyal subjects of the Queen of Heaven.

Here, on a festival like the one which I describe, one can see how deeply implanted devotion to the Blessed Virgin is in the inhabitants of this island of saints. It is as essential a constituent of their character as the soul is of the human being.

At the gable of the apparition, a life-size statue of Our Lady of Knock, is erected upon the spot where she stood on the evening of the 21st August of last year. The statue, which is the gift of some anonymous loving client of Mary, is carved in the best Portland stone, and costs about £40 or £50. I saw it placed in position on Friday last.

During the past ten days, the gable has been newly cemented, and it is expected that soon an iron railing will be built in front of it.

On the eve of the 8th, two paintings of exquisite workmanship, the Sacred Heart of Jesus, and the Immaculate Conception, are suspended, one over the vestry door, and the other over the statue of Our Lady of Lourdes. They were painted in Rome, by the special artist of the Jesu.

Indeed, hardly a single sun has set since the appearance of the Blessed Virgin here, accompanied by St. Joseph and St. John the Evangelist, that has not witnessed the advent of some token, more or less valuable, of the love borne to the Blessed Virgin by her Irish children, scattered as they are, throughout the whole world.

In an edition of "The Irish Times", dated Tuesday, October 12th, 1880, there is a report of a visit to Knock, which has been written by a Special Correspondent of "The Daily News". The report is compiled in the town of Claremorris.

The following is a very brief extract taken from the report:

"The favourite spot for the devotions outside is, of course, in front of the southern gable of the church..This wall, from which on my former visit nearly all the mortar had been removed by the pilgrims, has been repaired, and a substantial railing erected in front of it, to save the new plaster from the fate which befell the old....."

Mother Teresa enters the Apparition Church.

Mother Teresa at prayer in the Apparition Chapel.

Mother Teresa of Calcutta attending Mass at outdoor altar in Knock.

Thousands flocked to greet Mother Teresa in Knock during her visit.

IN ITS OWN GOOD TIME

God plants
In the famished land,
A seed;
To grow to fulness,
In its own good time.

In His wisdom,
A barren land He chooses,
To plant and cultivate.
Peasant hearts
Of no account ,
His choice of helper.
Can anything good come forth from
Such wretchedness?
Thus speaks the world !

And yet,
Even as the mustard seed,
This land has come to blossom,
Flowering forth,
Magnificent!

As the rose
Fair flowering,
Bursting forth
In petalled loveliness,
Mary's land is blooming,
In readiness for the picking:
As a fountain,
Ever gushing forth,
Resplendent,
Beautiful as Springtime,
Land of light:
As a volcano,
Whose first feeble sparks are
Insignificant,
But which ere long become
An inferno
Lighting the landscape.

As the tide,
That ever cometh
Surer,
Stronger,
Fuller,
Filling,
Overwhelming;
Receding now,
Then onward ever moving:
God's watered land of Knock.

Time proveth,
He knows best in His heaven,
And man liveth with his
foolishness.

TOM NEARY

Pilgrims getting Holy Water from font at Knock Shrine

CHAPTER 15
As the Rose Fair Flowering

1828—* Fr. Patrick O'Grady authorises the laying of foundations of Knock parish church.

1830—* Knock parish church is completed and dedicated to St. John the Baptist. An inscription placed on its west wall reads:"My house shall be called the house of prayer to all nations."

1879—* The Apparition at Knock, on the Thursday evening of August 21st.
     * An ecclesiastical Commission of inquiry is established by His Grace the Archbishop of Tuam, Most Rev. Dr. John MacHale.
     * The Commission's final verdict is that the testimony of all the witnesses taken as a whole is trustworthy and satisfactory.

1935—* Knock Shrine Society of Stewards and Handmaids is established with the approval of His Grace, the Archbishop of Tuam, Most Rev. Dr. T.P. Gilmartin. The founders are Mr. and Mrs. L. Coyne.

1936—* A second Commission of inquiry is established by His Grace the Archbishop of Tuam, Most Rev. Dr. T.P. Gilmartin.
     * The surviving witnesses confirm the evidence they gave to the first Commission.
     * The evidence of the witnesses together with statements from persons claiming substantial cure are submitted to Rome.

1938—* Outdoor Stations of Cross are erected.

1940—* Erection of Oratory at the Apparition Gable.

1950—* The proclamation of the Dogma of the Assumption, in St. Peter's, Rome, by His Holiness Pope Pius XII.

1954—* The blessing and decoration of the banner of Knock by His Holiness, Pope Pius XII, in St. Peter's basilica, Rome, on the occasion of the proclamation of the new feast of the Queenship of Mary.
     * The solemn crowning of the processional statue of Our Lady of Knock by kind permission of the Vatican Chapter.

1957—* The Church of the Apparition at Knock becomes an affiliated church of the basilica of St. Mary Major in Rome.
     * Special indulgences are granted to the stewards and handmaids of Knock Shrine Society and to all pilgrims visiting the shrine, by the Sacred Apostolic Penitentiary, at the request of His Grace the Archbishop of Tuam, Most Rev. Dr. Joseph Walsh.

1960—* His Holiness Pope John XXIII blesses and presents a beautiful candle to the shrine of Knock as being one of the most outstanding places of public devotion to the Blessed Virgin Mary.

1964—* At the end of the third session of the Second Vatican Council, His Holiness Pope Paul VI celebrates Mass in St. Peter's basilica with the custodians of the most famous Marian Shrines in the world. His Grace, the Archbishop of Tuam, Most Rev. Dr. Joseph Walsh, who is custodian of the shrine of Our Lady of Knock is one of the concelebrating bishops.

1968—* The Processional Square is developed.

1971—* St. Joseph's Rest House- residential hostel for invalids -is opened.

1974—* Knock Shrine Calvary is constructed on the Hill.

* Foundation stone of the great new church is blessed by His Holiness Pope Paul VI.

*The stone is laid by His Grace, the Archbishop of Tuam, Most Rev. Dr. Joseph Cunnane. It bears the inscription "Pope Paul VI" in large blue lettering on a background of white Carrara marble.

1976—* The new church (capacity 20,000) is blessed and dedicated to Our Lady Queen of Ireland, by His Grace the Archbishop of Tuam, Most Rev. Dr. Joseph Cunnane, assisted by the archbishops of Ireland and in the presence of His Eminence the late William Cardinal Conway, Archbishop of Armagh and Primate of All Ireland.

1978—* St. John's Rest-and-Care Centre is opened.

1979—* Knock Shrine Centenary Year.

* The church of Our Lady Queen of Ireland is consecrated on the 25th March, feast of the Annunciation.

* A National Missionary Congress is held at Knock in April to which His Holiness, Pope John Paul ll sends a special videotaped message.

* The special ceremonies marking the Centenary of the Apparition at Knock are held on the 15th August, feast of the Assumption of Our Lady. They are attended by Church and State dignitaries from all over the world.

* On Sunday, 30th September, 1979, His Holiness, Pope John Paul ll comes as a humble pilgrim to Knock Shrine where he is greeted by well-nigh half a million people.

* The Holy Father lays his hands upon the Sick and blesses them in the Basilica of Our Lady Queen of Ireland. In his address to them, he says: "Dear brothers and sisters,

The Gospels are filled with instances where Our Lord shows his particular love and concern for the sick and for all those in pain. Jesus loved those who suffered, and this attitude has been passed on to his Church. To love the sick is something that the Church has learned from Christ.

Today I am happy to be with the sick and the handicapped. I have come to give witness to Christ's love for you, and to tell you that the Church and the Pope love you too. They reverence and esteem you. They are convinced that there is something very special about your mission in the Church.

By his suffering and death Jesus took on himself all human suffering, and he gave it a new value. As a matter of fact, he calls upon the sick, upon everyone who suffers, to collaborate with him in the salvation of the world.

Because of this, pain and sorrow are not endured alone or in vain. Although it remains difficult to understand suffering, Jesus has made it clear that its value is linked to his own suffering and death, to his own sacrifice. In other words, by your suffering you help Jesus in his work of salvation. This great truth is difficult to express accurately, but Saint Paul puts it this way: "... in my flesh I complete what is lacking in Christ's afflictions for the sake of his body, that is, the Church" (Col 1: 24).

Your call to suffering requires strong faith and patience. Yes, it means that you are called to love with a special intensity. But remember that Our Blessed Mother, Mary, is close to you, just as she was close to Jesus at the foot of the cross. And she will never leave you all alone."

* Pope John Paul ll addresses the Handmaids and Stewards of Knock Shrine and the Directors of pilgrimages:

"Dear brothers and sisters in the Lord, As a pastor I feel in my heart a special joy in addressing a few words also to the handmaids and stewards of the Knock Shrine Society and to the directors of pilgrimages of Cnoc Mhuire, the Mountain of Mary.

The Eucharistic celebration of this afternoon brings back happy memories of the many pilgrimages in which I took part in my homeland at the Shrine of Jasna Gora, the Bright Mountain, in Czestochowa and at the other sites throughout Poland; it also recalls my visit to the Shrine of Our Lady of Guadalupe in Mexico.

I know from firsthand experience the value of the services you render to make every pilgrim feel at home at this Shrine, and to help them to make every visit a loving and prayerful encounter with Mary, the Mother of Divine Grace. In a special way, you are the servants of the Mother of Jesus. You help people to approach her, to receive her message of love and dedication, and to entrust to her their whole lives so that they may be true witnesses to the love of her Son. You are also servants of your brothers and sisters. In helping and guiding the many pilgrims and especially the sick and handicapped, you perform not only a work of charity but also a task of evangelisation. May this insight be your inspiration and your strength in order that all the tasks that you so generously accept to perform may become a living witness for the word of God and for the good tidings of salvation.

I pray for you, I thank you, and I invoke upon you abundant graces of goodness and holiness of life. Receive the blessing which I cordially extend to you and all your loved ones."

* Pope John Paul ll honours the Handmaids and Stewards of Knock Shrine by requesting that a Spiritual Bouquet, presented to him by them, should be kept always at the Shrine as a tribute to their faith and loyalty to the Holy See.

* His Holiness celebrates Mass at a specially constructed Altar between the Basilica and the Church of the Apparition. During the Mass he anoints the Sick. In the course of his Homily he says: "Sé do bheatha a Mhuire, atá lán de ghrásta...

Dear brothers and sisters in Christ, faithful sons and daughters of Mary."Here I am at the goal of my journey to Ireland: the Shrine of Our Lady at Knock. Since I first learnt of the Centenary of this Shrine... I have felt a strong desire to come here, the desire to make yet another pilgrimage to the Shrine of the Mother of Christ, the Mother of the Church, the Queen of Peace... Do we not confess with all our brethren, even with those with whom we are not yet linked in full unity, that we are a pilgrim people...

I am here then as a pilgrim, a sign of the pilgrim Church throughout the world participating, through my presence as Peter's successor, in a very special way in the centenary celebration of this Shrine. The Liturgy of the Word of today's Mass gives me my pilgrim's salutation to Mary, as now I come before her in Ireland's Marian Shrine at Cnoc Mhuire, the Hill of Mary...

Blessed are you among women, and blessed is the fruit of your womb", this is also my greeting to Mhuire Máthair Dé, Mary, the Mother of God, Queen of Ireland, at this Shrine of Knock. With these words, l want to express the immense joy and gratitude that fills my heart today in this place. l would not have wanted it any differently. Highlights of my recent pastoral journeys have been the visits to the Shrines of Mary: To Our Lady of Guadalupe in Mexico, to the Black Madonna of Jasna Gora in my homeland, and three weeks ago to Our Lady of Loreto in Italy. Today I come here because I want all of you to know that my devotion to Mary unites me, in a very special way, with the people of Ireland...

It is fitting then, and it gives me great happiness to see, that the Irish people maintain this traditional devotion to the Mother of

God in their homes and their parishes, and in a special way at this Shrine of Cnoc Mhuire. For a whole century now, you have sanctified this place of pilgrimage through your prayers, through your sacrifices, through your penance. All those who have come here have received blessings through the intercession of Mary. From that Day of Grace, the twenty-first of August, 1879, until this very day, the sick and suffering, people handicapped in body or mind, troubled in their faith or their conscience, all have been healed, comforted and confirmed in their faith because they trusted that the Mother of God would lead them to her Son, Jesus. Every time a pilgrim comes up to what was once an obscure bogside village in County Mayo, every time a man, woman or child comes up to the old Church with the Apparition Gable or to the new Shrine of Mary Queen of Ireland, it is to renew his or her faith in salvation that comes through Jesus, who made us all children of God and heirs to the Kingdom of Heaven. By entrusting yourselves to Mary, you receive Christ. In Mary, "The Word was made Flesh": in her the Son of God became man, so that all of us might know how great our human dignity is. Standing on this hallowed ground, we look up to the Mother of God and say—
" Blessed are you among women, and blessed is the fruit of your womb . "

* At the end of his Homily, Pope John Paul ll consecrates Ireland and her people to Mary Mother of the Church for it was in her role as Mother of the Church that she appeared at Knock in 1879. This Act of Consecration is, therefore, very significant. Here I quote a short extract from it:

"Mother, in this Shrine you gather the people of God of all Ireland and constantly point out to them Christ in the Eucharist and in the Church. At this solemn moment we listen with particular attention to your words: 'Do whatever my Son tells you', and we wish to respond to your words with all our hearts. We wish to do what your Son tells us, what he commands us, for he has the words of eternal life. We wish to carry out and fulfil all that comes from him, all that is contained in the good news, as our forefathers did for many centuries. Their fidelity to Christ and to his Church and their heroic attachment to the Apostolic See, have in a way stamped on all of us an indelible mark that we all share...

Today therefore, on the occasion of the first visit of a Pope to Ireland, we entrust and consecrate to you, Mother of the Church, our hearts, our consciences, and our work, in order that they may be in keeping with the faith we profess. We entrust and consecrate to you each and everyone of those who make up both the community of the Irish people and the community of the people of God living in this land...

Queen of Ireland, Mary Mother of the heavenly and earthly church, Máthair Dé, keep Ireland true to her spiritual tradition and her christian heritage. Help her to respond to her heroic mission of bringing the light of Christ to the nations, and so making the glory of God be the honour of Ireland." Referring to the problem of violence in Northern Ireland, His Holiness says: "Mother, can we keep silent about what we find most painful, what leaves us many a time so helpless? *In a very special way we entrust to you this great wound now afflicting our people, hoping that your hands will be able to cure and heal it . . . . ."* "A Mhuire na nGrás, a Mháthair Mhic Dé, go gcuirfidh tú ar mo leas mé."

* The Holy Father raises the Church of Our Lady Queen of Ireland to the status of Basilica in order to honour Our Lady of Knock in her Centenary Year.

* The highlight of the Holy Father's visit to Knock is when he kneels in silent prayer at the Apparition Gable, the very spot where the heavenly vision was witnessed a hundred years before.

* His Holiness blesses the Shrine statuary which depicts, in every detail, the Apparition scene of August 21st, 1879.

* The Holy Father lights a candle at the Apparition Gable to stress the importance of Family Prayer in the home. The place could not have been more appropriate for this gesture, for it was on that very spot where Our Lady led her own family in prayer: Jesus, the Lamb of God, Joseph and St. John, into whose care she was given on Calvary.

* Pope John Paul presents as his own personal gifts to the Shrine, a beautiful candle and a Rose in Gold to be kept as a memento of his visit and as a token of his approval of the wonderful work carried out there. With the latter gift, the church sets the seal on Knock, for all time, and places it among the greatest Marian shrines in the world.

1983—* The Blessed Sacrament Chapel is opened for daily Adoration during the pilgrimage season.

1984—* St. Brigid's Hostel is completed and brought into use.

1985—*Knock Shrine Society celebrates its Golden Jubilee.

*The inaugural flights from the new Knock Airport—Connaught Regional—Horan International—to Rome.

* The Golden Jubilee Pilgrimage of Knock Shrine Society to Rome, San Giovanni, Assisi and Loreto, coinciding with the inaugural flights from Knock Airport.

1987—* The new Folk Museum is opened.

1987—* On the occasion of the opening of the Marian Year, Knock Shrine is involved in a unique live television link-up by satellite with Rome and fifteen of the world's biggest Marian Shrines. The viewing audience is one billion.

1988—* A special ceremony to mark the closing of the Marian Year in Ireland is held at Knock Shrine on the 15th August and is attended by His Excellency the Papal Nuncio to Ireland, Most Rev. Dr. Gaetano Alibrandi, His Eminence Cardinal Tomás O Fiaich and the entire Irish Hierarchy.

* The 50th Edition of "Knock Shrine Annual" is published.

1990—* On July 15th, 1990 the Ceremony of Dedication takes place in the new Chapel of Reconciliation. The Chief Celebrant is Most Rev. Dr. Joseph Cassidy, Archbishop of Tuam and the Presiding Prelate is His Excellency, Archbishop Emmanuele Gerada, Apostolic Nuncio to Ireland. The Architects are Mr. John Meagher and Mr. Shane de Blacam.

This chapel is a place for quiet reflection, a place where pilgrims can receive the Sacrament of Penance in the best possible environment, in the presence of the Blessed Sacrament and a place where expert counselling is available to those who need it.

It is a tribute to the skills and vision of people in the architectural and building profession. It is also a monument to the faith and generosity of many of God's pilgrim people.

1992—* On May 10th, 1992, the new Apparition Chapel is formally dedicated by the Archbishop of Tuam, Most Rev. Dr. Joseph Cassidy. Speaking at the dedication ceremony, he says that it is 'one of the most functional, inventive and imaginative buildings that I have ever seen.' Monsignor Grealy, P.P., V.G., calls it 'an architectural gem which answers all the problems we had.' The architect is Polish born Mr. Andrzej Wejchert.

The Chapel frames the Apparition Gable and has as its centrepiece the magnificent white Carrara marble statuary which is an exact representation of the Apparition as described by the witnesses. It was designed and carved around 1960 in Rome by the gifted Roman sculptor Professor Ferri.

1993—* On the 5th June, 1993 Mother Teresa of Calcutta comes on pilgrimage to Knock Shrine.

* Mother Teresa visits the Apparition Chapel and prays there for some time.

* She is driven through the Processional Square in front of the Apparition Chapel where 50,000 pilgrims are assembled to give her a tumultuous welcome.

* On entering the basilica, she pays a short visit to the Blessed Sacrament Chapel and is then introduced to the thousands of invalids in the Basilica and welcomed to Knock by Rt. Rev. Msgr. Dominick Grealy, Parish Priest of Knock and Director of Knock Shrine.

* Mother Teresa addresses the assembled multitude from the Altar of the Basilica. Here are just a couple of brief extracts from her moving and meaningful talk:

* "Let us ask Our Lady to give us her heart, so beautiful, so pure, so immaculate; her heart is so full of love and humility. Let us ask that we may be able to receive Jesus the Bread of Life, love Him as she loved Him, serve Him as she served Him in the distressing disguise of the poorest of the poor. Jesus came to give us the Good News that God loves us, and that He wants us to love one another as He loves each one of us. To make it easy for us to love one another, He said 'Whatsoever you do to the least, you do it to Me'."

* "Families that pray together, stay together, and if we stay together we will love one another as God loves each one of us, because the fruit of prayer is a deepening of faith, and the fruit of faith is love, and the fruit of love is service, and the fruit of service is peace. God bless you."

* Following her address, Mother Teresa goes to the outdoor altar in

God bless you."

* Following her address, Mother Teresa goes to the outdoor altar in the tower wall at the front of the Basilica. Coming into view of the massive gathering on this beautiful sunny day, she receives a rousing Céad Míle Fáilte. The atmosphere is electric, colourful, banner-filled.

* From the outdoor altar of the Basilica, Mother Teresa recites her "Rosary for Life" with marvellous reflections before each decade. One of her reflections is as follows:-

* "Jesus rises to new life. Life is a precious gift of God, especially the life of the unborn child. He or she is a living member of the human race, like you and me, created in the image and likeness of God, for greater things, to love and to be loved. We pray, to Our Lady that all may come to realise that no church, no government or mother has the right to kill the unborn child, at any stage of its conception . . .

* Mary is united with Jesus forever. Jesus in the Bread of Life is our source of unity. Adoration of the Blessed Sacrament is a beautiful means of coming to the feet of Jesus, to heal our brokenness, our lack of love, our lack of forgiveness. Let us pray specially that unity may be restored to those families who are broken and that the leaders of our country may always protect and safeguard the sacredness of married life by never allowing divorce."

* Mother Teresa then attends Concelebrated Mass at the outdoor altar during which the Archbishop of Tuam, Most Rev. Dr. Joseph Cassidy, in his Homily, pays her a special tribute:-

"Mother Teresa of Calcutta, you remind us of many things and challenge us to great things. In all sorts of ways you are the conscience of the world. We thank you for visiting us in Ireland and at Knock. We salute the work you do, the work of your missionaries of charity and of like minded people all over the world. It is our privilege today to return in some measure the love you lavish on others.That we gladly do now: You have changed our lives! You have raised our sights! What you have done for the poor is an enrichment for all of us. Grow older – very, very slowly! We all need you. Though – for what you have done for the dying – you will never die! Thank you again and God Bless you."

O DAY OF GRACE

O Day of Grace and angels' wings,
When Heaven's light shone in our land!
A poor church gable on a hill,
The Virgin's place of vision grand.
Our Lady of Knock, Sweet Mystic Rose!
O Queen of Ireland, praise to thee!
When trials and troubles weighed us down,
You deigned to come and set us free.

CHORUS

O hail! O hail! Bright Sun of our Race!
O hail! O hail! O hail Full of Grace!

A golden crown gleamed on thy head,
And on thy brow a full-bloom rose;
White-robed you stood in silent prayer,
For our forebears in sorrow's throes.
O Mary wrapt in love's amaze,
Before God's holy throne above!
You came a Mother to us all,
To share with us your peace and love.

CHORUS

The saints were with you on that eve,
Your guardian Joseph there enshrined;
Sweet Spouse and Patron of the Church,
The layman great to thee inclined.
Loved John the preacher-bishop came,
The Gospel Book in hand to hold;
His message clear in symbols shone,
The Lamb will conquer he has told.

CHORUS

Upon an altar white and plain,
There stood the Lamb with Cross behind;
Bright wings of angels hovered 'round,
The risen Saviour of mankind.
O Mary Mother of the Church,
First flowering of the pilgrim flock!
Teach us to love and to adore,
The Lamb of God you brought to Knock.

CHORUS

Grey mists of evening gathered 'round,
And raindrops fell on grasses green;
But none fell where God's glory shone,
For Erin's children at the scene.
You came in glory Queen of Peace,
To give us hope through humble seers;
O teach us in your silence deep,
True meanings of our cross and tears!

CHORUS

Long years have passed since first you came,
That August evening in the rain;
But still we sense your presence near,
Your helping hand, the Lamb once slain.
O Mother gain for Ireland peace,
And for all nations worldwide!
Plead as at Cana's wedding feast,
For Christ will answer you his pride.

CHORUS

O Mary comfort and console,
The Sick who gather 'round your Shrine!
And bring the healing hand of Christ,
To touch them as in Palestine.
Our Lady of Knock through Him you cure,
The crippled walk and blind men see;
Your prayers to Jesus reconcile,
And change our hearts to love for thee.

CHORUS

The Faith we kept, our treasure proud,
By Mass Rocks bare in Penal Days;
The beads we told in cabins poor,
To light our dark and troubled ways.
O Mary grant us still to share,
The Lamb's own marriage feast with thee!
Help us to pray as you have prayed,
And in our homes our Mother be.

CHORUS

Accept, O Mother, as our gifts,
Fresh flowers that bloom in summertime;
Bright beads of Aves from the heart,
Sweet songs of praise and bells that chime.
Take these, the tokens of our love,
Fresh-tinged by strands of candlelight,
And when we've walked our pilgrim road,
Lead us to Christ in mansions bright.

CHORUS

Tom Neary

133.

GOD'S WAY

The massive spreading pile,
On the hill,
Circular;
Hugging, as it were, this patch of earth.
A concrete colossus,
Pressing down;
Steel—strengthened,
Permanent.
Our Lady's basilica,
Refuge of the poor,
Raised up where the humble cottage stood,
Home of heavenly favour.

Where once the Byrne children played,
The thousands pray,
Their voices high
Sweetly singing
"Immaculate".
Our Lady, Queen of Ireland,
Borne 'round in endless procession,
Flower-bedecked.
The crown.

Penitent files.
The Way of the Cross.
Eucharistic celebration.
Ceremonial colourful,
Banner-filled.
Anointing,
Receiving,
Blessing.
The Lamb of God,
Health restoring.
Invalid lines,
Suppliant,
Silent,
'Live with joyous hope.
A holy city,
Where princes walk the peasant
ground,
And papal honour bold is writ.

Above—
A slender steeple in the clouds.
Abroad—
The stone of Ireland.

Thatch and whitewash,
Chimney-smoke.
Nothingness!
Greatness!
God's way.
Nazareth,
Bethlehem,
Knock.
God's way - confounding.

TOM NEARY

Basilica of Our Lady
Queen of Ireland.

CHAPTER 16
The Riches of Knock

The Apparition at Knock is a fountain filled with eternal riches and good things for mankind in an uncertain world of many misfortunes.

It testifies to the truth and the reality of the Gospel Story, and its language is the language of silent symbolism, a medium of communication superior to any words. By means of this language it speaks to the heart. The more one thinks about it, the clearer does its meaning and message become.

Let us then draw out of the riches of Knock something of that meaning and message in order that we may better appreciate and understand the significance of that August evening in 1879.

Our Lady appears attired as a queen with her brilliant and sparkling crown. Here we see the queen of Heaven asserting the truth of her coronation. She is already crowned as queen of the church in Heaven and she would have us see that this is really so. By coming to Knock she would have us see also that she is queen of the church on earth. Because of her queenship, she has a special responsibility for the human race. We are all her children. She cares for each and every one, especially for her suffering and sinful children. It is because she cares she comes to show her concern and she comes to Knock because no nation has been more loyal to her Crown of Roses. Because of her queenship, it is our duty to pay her homage, reverence and respect. Her role as queen is universal in the scheme of God and for this reason homage, reverence and respect are due to her in all lands and at all times.

Mary appears at Knock wearing her crown which presupposes her glorious assumption. She comes to Knock within the octave of the Feast of the Assumption. She comes from Heaven to clarify, for all time, the fact and reality of her assumption, which in 1879, has not been proclaimed a Dogma of the universal church.

Mary is assumed into Heaven and there crowned queen because she has shared in the work of our Redemption.

All these things are possible only because, first and foremost, Mary is chosen as God's Mother and later as our mother, too. Knock is a reminder of her universal motherhood, a reminder of salvation day on Calvary. On that day "when Jesus saw his mother, and the disciple, whom he loved standing near, he said to his mother, 'Woman, behold, your son!' Then he said to the disciple, 'Behold, your mother!' And from that hour the disciple took her to his own home." (John 19).

At Knock, Mary and John stand, side by side, in the presence of the Cross, standing upright on an altar with the Lamb of God. Because of Our Lady's motherhood, the world is given a saviour, Jesus Christ, the Lamb of God who takes away the sins of the world. She gives us her Son for our salvation and shares in our salvation with him. At Knock, Mary would have us reflect upon the implications of her motherly role, the incarnation and the drama of our salvation. She would have us appreciate the value of these mysteries, pondering them in our hearts.

At Knock, Mary's hands and eyes are raised up in prayer. Doubtless, her prayer is for that church of which she is the mother. She is the first redeemed, the first flowering of the pilgrim church. Her prayer is for all her children, especially for those most in need. As mother of the universal church she would have us understand the necessity of prayer in our lives and the efficacy of that same prayer especially when it is made through her who appears as our intercessor and helper. Prayer leads to glory and to the enjoyment of all good things.

The church is a universal family made up of countless individual family units. Knock is a reminder of the importance of the Christian family and the good home. The Holy Family is present—Mary, Joseph and the Lamb. Here, Mary is mother of the universal family. Joseph is patron of the universal family. The Lamb is the saviour of the universal family. Mary would have us learn at Knock the lessons of the family home of Nazareth.

St. John the Evangelist appears at Knock as the universal preacher. He represents the official teaching church. The beloved disciple also represents the ministerial church, the priesthood, empowered to offer the Eucharistic celebration, which is Calvary continued and renewed, until the end of time. Mary would have us learn at Knock, respect for and acceptance of, the word of God, which St. John holds in the open book, in his left hand. She would have us respect, too, the preachers and teachers of that word.

The vision of Knock is a consolation in hungry times but it is also a pointer to a deeper and more lasting hunger in mankind, a hunger which can only be satisfied by a spiritual food, namely, the Blessed Eucharist, the Bread of Life. In 1879 there are blighted fields in Ireland but they too are outward signs of a more destructive blight, which kills the soul—the blight of sin and wrongdoing. The Irish people fight for their land but Knock reminds them of another land, the possession of which is all that really matters. It is a guarantee of the resurrection and the reality of Heaven and as such is a source of unending joy, a beacon of Christian hope.

Our pilgrim journey to glory is made possible at Knock for Mary would have us avail of the fruits of the Incarnation and Redemption. She invites us to receive the Sacraments, and by receiving them, our eternal destiny is assured.

There is no other shrine in the world where the Sacraments may be received so readily and easily as at Knock. There is no other shrine in the world where the Sacraments are more valued and respected. This is Mary's way. She draws her children to her shrine and retiring into the background, hands them over to her Son.

In a very real sense, the hungry are fed with the Bread of Life at Knock but not before they have made their peace with God and are in his friendship. This takes place in and through a good confession. The reconciling of souls to God is at the very heart of any understanding of the true nature and message of Knock. It is at Knock that those hungry in spirit are fed. It is at Knock that those who are blighted in spirit are restored to a new life and a new relationship with God, the father of creation. This work must be dear to the heart of Mary at Knock.

The physical miracles and cures of Knock, wonderful as they are, are assurances for all of us, of that more wondrous spiritual healing which is the ongoing task of Knock. It is true to say also that the physical wonders, particularly numerous in the early years, point, on the one hand, to the divine origin of Knock, and, on the other, to its not so obvious but more urgent spiritual wonders.

In the Apparition at Knock there stands a cross upon the altar of the Lamb. It is a reminder of the value of suffering and the reward for bearing it well. At Knock the sick are given an appreciation of their vocation and an understanding of its immeasurable merits. Not infrequently is the cross lifted from the bruised and broken bodies and to all the afflicted is given strength, hope, resignation and consolation. The graces and blessings of God come to them, in and through the Sacrament of the Anointing, the Blessing of the Sick and the Bread of Strength.

The Apparition at Knock is rich in the mysteries of God, the mysteries of the Rosary. We can do no better than reflect upon them as we recite Our Lady's own beloved prayer. The beautiful full-blown rose on her brow is a call to pray her Crown of Roses and in so doing to reflect upon the mysteries of Redemption. She is the Mystic Rose pondering in her heart, the mysteries of God, in the silence of Knock—Immaculate, Seat of Wisdom. She would have us draw near that we might listen and in listening understand:

"Approach me, you who desire me, and take your fill of my fruits, for memories of me are sweeter than honey, inheriting me is sweeter than the honeycomb. They who eat me will hunger for more, they who drink me will thirst for more. Whoever listens to me will never have to blush, whoever acts as I dictate will never sin."

If we would enjoy the friendship of the Father from whence comes Peace—the peace of the beatitudes—let us open our hearts and minds to the vision and apostolates of Knock.

It is this peace that the pilgrim of Knock seeks and so often finds—an interior calm— an extreme happiness.

There is the beatitude of the poor who leave this blessed place in the certainty of the Kingdom. There is the beatitude of those who mourn but who have found their comforter. There is the beatitude of those who had hunger and thirst for justice but who leave satisfied. There is the beatitude of the merciful whose mercy has won for them mercy in return..........

Poor and pure children, on their knees, on the wet meadow grass by the Gable, their faces held towards the Mother of God, on a Mayo hill.. Let us look at this scene one last time, before leaving Knock. Let us carry it to the depths of our hearts: the entire meaning and message of Knock is contained in its light, by the church of St. John the Baptist. It was of him that St. John the Evangelist wrote: "He was not the Light, but a witness of the Light". The poor and pure of Knock are, likewise, witnesses of the Light, and who can deny that they are saints?

Knock, sanctuary of love! The love of the Beloved Disciple.

Knock, sanctuary of hope! The hope of the risen Lamb.

Knock, sanctuary of faith! The faith of her whom we especially honour as Our Lady of Knock.

"O God you are the Father of the poor and the support of the humble. When dangers surround your people you strengthen them by the protection of the Blessed Virgin Mary. Grant that through her prayers for us, as our Mother, we may follow the way of the Gospel and serve you with joy in our hearts by loving our brother for your sake. Through Our Lord Jesus Christ, your Son, who lives and reigns with you in the unity of the Holy Spirit, God, for ever and ever. Amen."

(Prayer: Mass of Our Lady of Knock)

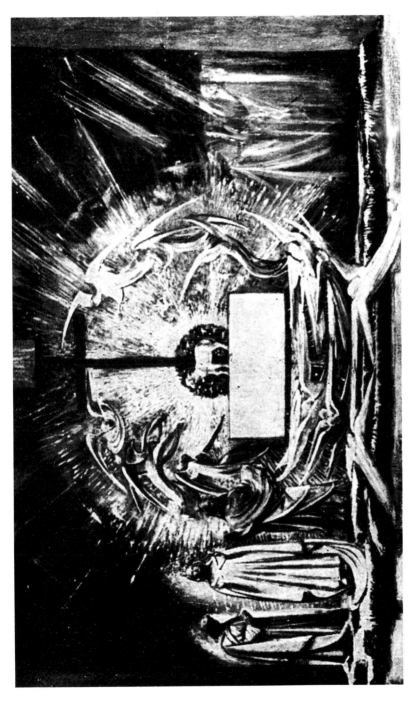

An artist's impression of the Apparition at Knock, Thursday Evening, August 21st, 1879 *-Ferri-Roma.*

Appendices

Appendix I

BRIDGET TRENCH'S KNOCK

Little green fields and brown,
Hill and hollow,
Simple scenes.
Tiny whitewashed cottages,
Dispersed.
Bridget Trench's Knock.

Scents
Of the rural West:
The soil,
At ploughing time;
Heather perfume,
Carried in the wind;
Newly cut
Grasses.

Haycocks
At haytime.
Turf stacks and
Moorland.
Oats
In the haggard.

Sounds
Of the farmyard:
Barking and
Lowing
Hens
With their chickens,
Crowding the doorway.

The bell of the Angelus,
Noonday and
Evening;
Cnoc Mhuire folk's
Gaelic,
A prayer on their lips.

At ease with
Their little;
Homely and happy;
Blessing the days with
The beads
On their breasts.

   - TOM NEARY

Appendix II THE FIFTEEN DEPOSITIONS

Shortly after the Apparition, His Grace, the Archbishop of Tuam, Most Rev. Dr. John MacHale, appoints an ecclesiastical Commission to see into the truth of the vision, as the parish of Knock is within the Archdiocese of Tuam. The members of the Commission of inquiry are: Very Rev. Archdeacon Bartholomew A. Cavanagh, P.P.; Rev. James Canon Waldron, P.P., Ballyhaunis; and Rev. Ulick J. Canon Bourke, P.P., Kilcolman, Claremorris, Co. Mayo.

Fifteen witnesses come before the Commission and give their evidence. The number includes men, women, teenagers and children of various ages. Patrick Hill is 11 years of age; Mary McLoughlin is about 45; Mary Byrne (later Mrs. O'Connell, is 29; Patrick Walsh is about 65; Patrick Byrne is 16; Mrs. Margaret Byrne is 68; Dominick Byrne, Junior is 18 to 20; Mrs. Hugh Flatley is 44; Bridget Trench is 74 to 75; Catherine Murray is $8^3/_4$; John Curry is $5^1/_2$; Judith Campbell is 22; Margaret Byrne is 21; Dominick Byrne, Senior is 36 and John Durkan is about 24.

One of the witnesses, namely Bridget Trench, speaks Gaelic fluently and it is in Gaelic that she gives her evidence. An English translation of her evidence is also included here.

All fifteen depositions appear in various editions of "The Weekly News" in the early part of the year 1880.

The following are the fifteen depositions as officially recorded by the Commissioners in 1879 and as published in the Press of the day:

PATRICK HILL

"I am Patrick Hill; I live in Claremorris; my aunt lives at Knock; I remember the 21st August last; on that day I was drawing home turf, or peat from the bog, on an ass.

While at my aunt's at about eight o'clock in the evening, Dominick Byrne came into the house; he cried out: 'Come up to the chapel and see the miraculous lights, and the beautiful visions that are to be seen there'.

I followed him; another man by name Dominick Byrne, and John Durkan, and a small boy named John Curry, came with me; we were all together; we ran over towards the chapel.

When we, running southwest, came so far from the village that on our turning, the gable came into view, we immediately beheld the lights; a clear white light, covering most of the gable, from the ground up to the window and higher. It was a kind of changing bright light, going sometimes up high and again not so high.

We saw the figures—the Blessed Virgin, St. Joseph and St. John, and an altar with a Lamb on the altar, and a cross behind the Lamb.

At this time we reached as far as the wall fronting the gable: there were other people there before me; some of them were praying, some not; all were looking at the vision; they were leaning over the wall or ditch, with their arms resting on the top.

I saw the figures and brightness; the boy, John Curry, from behind the wall could not see them; but I did; and he asked me to lift him up till he could see the grand babies, as he called the figures.

It was raining. Some, amongst them Mary McLoughlin, who beheld what I now saw, had gone away; others were coming.

After we prayed a while I thought it right to go across the wall and into the chapel yard. I brought little Curry with me; I went then up closer; I saw everything distinctly. The figures were full and round as if they had a body and life; they said nothing; but as we approached they seemed to go back a little towards the gable.

I distinctly beheld the Blessed Virgin Mary, life size, standing about two feet or so above the ground clothed in white robes which were fastened at the neck.

Her hands were raised to the height of the shoulders, as if in prayer, with the palms facing one another, but slanting inwards towards the face; the palms were not turned towards the people, but facing each other as I have described; she appeared to be praying; her eyes were turned as I saw towards heaven.

She wore a brilliant crown on her head, and over the forehead where the crown fitted the brow, a beautiful rose; the crown appeared brilliant, and of a golden brightness, of a deeper hue, inclined to a mellow yellow, than the striking whiteness of the robes she wore; the upper parts of the crown appeared to be a series of sparkles, or glittering crosses.

I saw her eyes, the balls, the pupils and the iris of each. (The boy did not know the special names of those parts of the eye, but he pointed to them, and described them in his own way).

I noticed her hands especially, and face, her appearance.

The robes came only as far as the ankles; I saw her feet and the ankles; one foot, the right, was slightly in advance of the other.

At times she appeared, and all the figures appeared, to move out and again to go backwards; I saw them move; she did not speak; I went up very near; one old woman went up and embraced the Virgin's feet, and she found nothing in her arms and hands; they receded, she said, from her.

I saw St. Joseph to the Blessed Virgin's right hand; his head was bent, from the shoulders, forward; he appeared to be paying his respects; I noticed his whiskers; they appeared slightly grey; there was a line or dark mearing between the figure of the Blessed Virgin and the spot where he stood. I saw the feet of St. Joseph, too. His hands were joined like a person at prayer.

The third figure that stood before me was that of St. John the Evangelist. He stood erect at the side of the altar, and at an angle with the figure of the Blessed Virgin, so that his back was not turned to the altar nor to the Mother of God. His right arm was at an angle with a line drawn across from St. Joseph to where Our Blessed Lady appeared to be standing.

St. John was dressed like a bishop preaching; he wore a small mitre on his head; he held a Mass Book, or a Book of Gospels, in his left hand; the right hand was raised to the elevation of the head; while he kept the index finger and the middle finger of the right hand raised; the other three fingers of the same hand were shut; he appeared as if he were preaching, but I heard no voice; I came so near that I looked into the book. I saw the lines and the letters. St. John did not wear any sandals.

His left hand was turned towards the altar that was behind him; the altar was a plain one, like any ordinary altar, without any ornaments.

On the altar stood a lamb, the size of a lamb eight weeks old—the face of the lamb was fronting the west, and looking in the direction of the Blessed Virgin and St. Joseph.

Behind the lamb a large cross was placed erect or perpendicular on the altar. Around the Lamb I saw angels hovering during the whole time, for the space of one hour and a half or longer; I saw their wings fluttering, but I did not perceive their heads or faces, which were not turned to me.

For the space of an hour and a half we were under the pouring rain; at this time I was very wet; I noticed that the rain did not wet the figures which appeared before me, although I was wet myself.

I went away then." October 8th, 1879.

MARY McLOUGHLIN

"I Mary McLoughlin, live in Knock; I am housekeeper to the Rev. Archdeacon Cavanagh.

I remember the evening of the 21st August; at the hour of seven or so or a little later, while it was yet bright day, I passed from the Rev. the Archdeacon's house on by the chapel, towards the house of Mrs. Byrne, widow.

On passing by the chapel, and at a little distance from it, I saw a wonderful number of strange figures or appearances at the gable; one like the Blessed Virgin Mary, and one like St. Joseph; another a bishop; I saw an altar.

I was wondering to see there such an extraordinary group; yet I passed on and said nothing, thinking that possibly the Archdeacon had been supplied with these beautiful figures from Dublin or somewhere else, and that he said nothing about them, but had left them in the open air; I saw a white light about them; I thought the whole thing strange.

After looking at them I passed on to the house of Mrs. Byrne's in the village; after reaching widow Byrne's house I stayed there half an hour at least.

I returned then homewards to the Archdeacon's house accompanied by Miss Mary Byrne, and as we approached the chapel, she cried out 'Look at the beautiful figures.'

We gazed at them for a little, and then I told her to go for her mother, widow Byrne, and her brother and her sister, and her niece who were still in the house which she and I had left.

I remained looking at the sight before me until the mother, sister, and brother of Mary Byrne came; at the time I was outside the ditch and to the south-west of the school-house near the road, about thirty yards or so from the church; I leaned across the wall in order to see, as well as I could, the whole scene. I remained now for the space of at least a quarter of an hour, perhaps longer.

I told Miss Byrne then to go for her uncle, Brian Byrne, and her aunt, Mrs. Brian Byrne, or any of the neighbours whom she should see, in order that they might witness the sight that they were then enjoying.

It was now about a quarter past eight o'clock, and beginning to be quite dark. The sun had set; it was raining at the time.

I beheld, on this occasion, not only the three figures, but an altar further on to the left of the figure of the Blessed Virgin Mary, and to the left of the bishop and above the altar a lamb about the size of that which is five weeks old. Behind the lamb appeared the cross; it was away a bit from the lamb, while the latter stood in front from it, and not resting on the wood of the cross. Around the lamb a number of gold-like stars appeared in the form of a halo.

This altar was placed right under the window of the gable and more to the east of the figures, all, of course, outside the church at Knock.

I parted from the company or gathering at eight and a half o'clock. I went to the priest's house and told what I had beheld, and spoke of the beautiful things that were to be seen at the gable of the chapel. I asked him or said, rather, it would be worth his while to go to witness them.

He appeared to make nothing of what I said, and consequently he did not go. Although it was pouring rain the wall had a bright, dry appearance, while the rest of the building appeared to be dark.

I did not return to behold the visions again after that, remaining at my house. I saw the sight for fully an hour.

Very Rev. B. Cavanagh heard the next day all about the apparition from the others who had beheld it; and then it came to his recollection that I had told him the previous evening about it, and asked him to see it".

MARY BYRNE

"I live in the village of Knock, to the east side of the chapel.

Mary McLoughlin came on the evening of the 21st August to my house at about half past seven o'clock. She remained some little time.

I came back with her as she was returning homewards. It was either eight o'clock or a quarter to eight at the time. It was still bright.

I had never heard from Miss McLoughlin about the vision which she had seen just before that.

The first I learned of it was on coming at the time just named from my mother's house in company with Miss Mary McLoughlin, and at the distance of three hundred yards or so from the church. I beheld, all at once, standing out from the gable, and rather to the west of it, three figures which, on more attentive inspection, appeared to be that of the Blessed Virgin, St. Joseph and St. John.

That of the Blessed Virgin was life-size, the others apparently either not so big or not so high as her figure.

They stood a little distance out from the gable wall, and, as well as I could judge, a foot and a half or two feet from the ground.

The Virgin stood erect, with eyes raised to heaven, her hands elevated to the shoulders or a little higher, the palms inclined slightly towards the shoulders or bosom. She wore a large cloak of a white colour, hanging in full folds and somewhat loosely around her shoulders, and fastened to the neck.

She wore a crown on the head, rather a large crown, and it appeared to me somewhat yellower than the dress or robes worn by Our Blessed Lady.

In the figure of St. Joseph the head was slightly bent, and inclined towards the Blessed Virgin, as if paying her respect. It represented the saint as somewhat aged, with grey whiskers and greyish hair.

The third figure appeared to be that of St. John the Evangelist. I do not know, only I thought so, except the fact that at one time I saw a statue at the chapel of Lecanvey, near Westport, Co. Mayo, very much resembling the figure which stood now before me in group with St. Joseph and Our Blessed Lady, which I beheld on this occasion.

He held the Book of Gospels, or the Mass Book, open in his left hand, while he stood slightly turned on the left side towards the altar that was over a little from him.

I must remark that the statue which I had formerly seen at Lecanvey chapel had no mitre on its head, while the figure which I now beheld had one, not a high mitre, but a short set kind of one.

The statue at Lecanvey had a book in the left hand, and the fingers of the right hand raised. The figure before me on this present occasion of which I am speaking had a book in the left hand, as I have stated, and the index finger and the middle finger of the right hand raised, as if he were speaking, and impressing some point forcibly on an audience.

It was this coincidence of figure and pose that made me surmise, for it is only an opinion, that the third figure was that of St. John, the beloved disciple of Our Lord, but I am not in any way sure what saint or character the figure represented. I said, as I now expressed, that it was St. John the Evangelist, and then all the others present said the same—said what I stated.

The altar was under the window, which is in the gable and a little to the west near the centre, or a little beyond it.

Towards this altar St. John, as I shall call the figure, was looking, while he stood at the Gospel side of the said altar, with his right arm inclined at an angle outwardly, towards the Blessed Virgin.

The altar appeared to me to be like the altars in use in the Catholic Church, large and full-sized. It had no linens, no candles, nor any special ornamentations; it was only a plain altar.

Above the altar and resting on it, was a lamb, standing with the face towards St. John, thus fronting the western sky.

I saw no cross or crucifix.

On the body of the lamb, and around it, I saw golden stars, or small brilliant lights, glittering like jets or glass balls, reflecting the light of some luminous body.

I remained from a quarter past eight to half past nine o'clock. At the time it was raining."

147.

PATRICK WALSH

"My name is Patrick Walsh; I live in Ballinderrig, an English mile from the chapel at Knock.

I remember well the 21st August, 1879. It was a very dark night. It was raining heavily.

About nine o'clock on that night I was going on some business through my land, and standing a distance of about half a mile from the chapel, I saw a very bright light on the southern gable end of the chapel; It appeared to me to be a large globe of golden light; I never saw, I thought, so brilliant a light before; it appeared high up in the air above and around the chapel gable and it was circular in its appearance; it was quite stationary, and it seemed to retain the same brilliancy all through.

The following day I made enquiries in order to learn if there were any lights seen in the place that night; it was only then I heard of the vision or apparitions that the people had seen. "

PATRICK BYRNE

"I am sixteen years of age; I live quite near the chapel; I remember well the evening of the 21st August; it was Thursday, the evening before the Octave day.

Dominick Byrne, junior, a namesake of mine, came to my house, and said that he had seen the biggest sight that ever he witnessed in his life. It was then after eight o'clock.

I came by the road on the west side of the church, I saw the figures clearly, fully, and distinctly, the Blessed Virgin, St. Joseph, and that of a bishop, said to be St. John the Evangelist. (Young Byrne then told what he saw regarding the vision, just as it has been described already by several persons who were present. The young fellow showed by his hands and position how the image or apparition of the Blessed Virgin Mary and that of St. Joseph and St. John stood).

I remained only ten minutes, and then I went away.

All this happened between a quarter or so past eight o'clock and half past nine."

MARGARET BYRNE (Widow)

"I, Margaret Byrne, nee Bourke, widow of Dominick Byrne, deceased, live near the chapel at Knock.

I remember the evening of the 21st August.

I was called out at about a quarter past eight o'clock by my daughter Margaret to see the vision of the Blessed Virgin Mary, and of the saints who appeared at the end of the little church.

It was getting dark; it was raining.

I came with others to the wall opposite the gable.

I saw then and there distinctly the three images, one of the Blessed Virgin Mary, one of St. Joseph, and the third, as I learned, that of St. John the Evangelist.

I saw an altar, too, and a lamb on it somewhat whiter than the altar; I did not see the cross on the altar.

The Blessed Virgin Mary appeared in the attitude of prayer, with her eyes turned up towards heaven, a crown on her head, and an outer garment thrown around her shoulders. I saw her feet.

St. Joseph appeared turned towards the Blessed Virgin, with head inclined. I remained looking on for fully fifteen or twenty minutes; then I left and returned to my own house."

DOMINICK BYRNE

"I am brother of Mary Byrne, who has given her evidence already; I live near the chapel of Knock. My age is twenty years.

On the occasion when my sister came about eight o'clock on the evening of the 21st of August into our house, she exclaimed: 'Come Dominick, and see the image of the Blessed Virgin, as she has appeared to us down at the chapel.' I said: What image?" and then she told me, as she has already described it for your Reverence in her testimony; she told me all she was after seeing.

I then went with her, and by this time some ten or twelve people had been collected around the place, namely, around the ditch or wall fronting the gable, where the vision was being seen, and to the south of the schoolhouse.

Then I beheld the three likenesses or figures that have been already described, the Blessed Virgin, St. Joseph, and St. John, as my sister called the bishop, who was like one preaching, with his hand raised towards the shoulder, and the forefinger and middle finger pointedly set, the other two fingers compressed by the thumb; in his left hand he held a book; he was so turned that he looked half towards the altar and half towards the people. The eyes of the images could be seen; they were like figures, inasmuch as they did not speak.

I was filled with wonder at the sight I saw; I was so affected that I shed tears.

I continued looking on for fully an hour, and then I went away to visit Mrs. Campbell, who was in a dying state.

When we returned the vision had disappeared."

MRS. HUGH FLATLEY

Mrs. Hugh Flatley, widow of Hugh Flatley, states:

"I was passing by the chapel of Knock on the evening of the 21st August, about eight o'clock, and I beheld most clearly and distinctly the figures of the Blessed Virgin Mary, St. Joseph, and that of St. John the Evangelist, standing erect at the gable end of the chapel, towards the south side.

I thought that the parish priest had been ornamenting the church, and got some beautiful likenesses removed outside."

BRÍD NÍ THRINSIGH

"Bríd Ní Thrinsigh is ainm dom; tá cónaí orm in aice an t-séipéil ar an gCnoc.

Timpeall leath uair tar éis a seacht ar oíche 21ú Lúnasa, bhíos i dteach

Bean Uí Chathmhaoil, atá cóngarach don séipéal; fad a bhíos ansin tháinig Máire Ní Bhroinn isteach agus dúirt sí go raibh radharc le feiceáil ag an séipéal nach bhfacamar riamh roimhe seo, agus dúirt sí linn teacht agus é a fheiceáil; d'fhiafraíos dí céard ab ea é, agus dúirt sí go raibh an Mhaighdean Bheannaithe, Naomh Íosaf agus Naomh Eoin le feiceáil ansin.

Chuas amach díreach agus thángas chomh fada leis an áit a bhí luaite.

Nuair a shroiceas an áit sin chonaiceas go soiléir na trí figiúirí; chaitheas mé féin síos ar mo ghlúna agus gháireas: "Céad míle buíochas le Dia agus leis an Maighdin ghlórmhair a thug dúinn an taispeánadh seo".

Chuas isteach díreach le cosa na Maighdine Muire a phógadh, mar a cheapas; ach níor mhothaíos tada i mo bharróig seachas an balla, agus rinneas iontas mar níor thuigeas an fáth nach rabhas ábalta mothú le mo lámha na figiúirí a bhí feicthe agam chomh soiléir agus chomh gléineach.

Bhí na trí figiúirí le feiceáil gan chorraí, dealbhach; bhíodar ina seasamh ag binn an t-séipéil ar a gcúl agus bhreathnaíodar ardaithe dhá throigh nó mar sin os cionn na talún.

Bhí an Mhaighdean Bheannaithe i lár báire; bhí culaith gheal uirthi agus bhí sí clúdaithe i mball éadaigh bháin amháin, de réir dealraimh; bhí a lámha ardaithe go dtí an suíomh céanna ina mbíonn lámha sagairt nuair a bhíonn sé ag guí ag Aifreann naofa. Shonraíos go gléineach codanna íochtaracha a cos, agus phógas iad trí huaire; bhí rud éigin ar a ceann cosúil le coróin, agus bhí a súile ardaithe i dtreo na nimhe. Bhíos chomh tógtha leis an Maighdin Bheannaithe nár thugas mórán aire d'éinne eile; mar sin féin chonaiceas chomh maith an dá fhigiúr eile, Naomh Íosaf ina sheasamh ar dheis na Maighdine Beannaithe nó ar chlé, mar a d'fhéachas féin air, a cheann claonta ina treo agus a lámha i gcomhar; agus an figiúir eile, a thógas mar Naomh Eoin, as Soiscéalaí, bhí sé ina sheasamh ar a clé. Chualas na daoine thart timpeall orm ag rá gurbh é íomhá Naoimh Eoin é.

Bhí sé ag cur fearthainne an-trom ag an am, ach níor thit aon bháisteach mar a raibh na figiúirí. Mhothaíos an talamh go cúramach le mo lámha agus bhí sé tirim ar fad. Bhí an ghaoth ag séideadh aneas, díreach in aghaidh beann an tséipéil, ach níor thit aon bháisteach ar an gcuid sin den bhinn nó séipéal ina raibh na figiúirí.

Ní raibh aon ghluaiseacht nó chomhartha gníomhach na beatha timpeall ar na figiúirí, agus ní bhéinn in ann a rá an rabhadar mar a shamhlódh daoine beo dá mbeidís ina n-áit nó nach raibh; ach do shamhlaíodar chomh lán agus chomh beoga agus ar thomhas nádúrtha nach rabhas in ann tuiscint an fáth nach rabhas ábalta iad a mhothú le mo lámha mar a bhfacas iad le mo shúile.

Bhí gile neamhchoitianta timpeall ar bhinn an t-séipéil uilig, agus chonaic a lán a bhí ag imeacht thart ar an mbóthar í ag an am.

D'fhanas ansin uair a'chloig ar fad, agus nuair a thángas ansin i dtosach cheapas nach bhfaighinn an áit go deo. Ní rachainn chomh túisce is a chuas ach mhacnaíos go leanfadh na figiúirí agus an ghile sin ansin i gcónaí agus ar theacht ar ais dom go bhfeicfinn arís iad.

Leanas ag athrá na Coróine Muire ar mo phaidrín fad a bhíos ansin agus mhothaíos an-aoibhneas agus pléisiúr is mé ag féachaint ar an Maighdin Bheannaithe. Ní rabhas in ann smaoineamh ar thada fad a bhíos ansin ach ag tabhairt buíochais le Dia ag athrá mo phaidreacha."

BRIDGET TRENCH

"My name is Bridget Trench; I live near the chapel at Knock.

About half past seven o'clock on the night of the 21st of August, I was in the house of Mrs. Campbell, which is quite near to the chapel; while I was there Mary Byrne came in and said there was a sight to be seen at the chapel such as we never before beheld, and she told us all to come and see it; I asked her what it was, and she said that the Blessed Virgin, St. Joseph and St. John were to be seen there.

I went out immediately and came to the spot indicated.

When I arrived there I saw distinctly the three figures; I threw myself on my knees and exclaimed: "A hundred thousand thanks to God and to the glorious Virgin that has given us this manifestation."

I went in immediately to kiss, as I thought, the feet of the Blessed Virgin; but I felt nothing in the embrace but the wall, and I wondered why I could not feel with my hands the figures which I had so plainly and so distinctly seen.

The three figures appeared motionless, statue-like; they were standing by the gable of the church in the background, and seemed raised about two feet above the ground.

The Blessed Virgin was in the centre; she was clothed in white, and covered with what appeared one white garment; her hands were raised to the same position as that in which a priest holds his hands when praying at holy Mass. I remarked distinctly the lower portions of her feet, and kissed them three times; she had on her head something resembling a crown, and her eyes were turned up heavenwards. I was so taken with the Blessed Virgin, that I did not pay much attention to any other; yet I saw also the two other figures, St. Joseph standing to the right of the Blessed Virgin, or to the left, as I looked at him, his head bent towards her and his hands joined; and the other figure, which I took to be St. John the Evangelist, was standing at her left. I heard those around me say that the image was St. John.

It was raining very heavily at the time, but no rain fell where the figures were. I felt the ground carefully with my hands and it was perfectly dry. The wind was blowing from the south, right against the gable of the chapel, but no rain fell on that portion of the gable or chapel in which the figures were.

There was no movement or active sign of life about the figures, and I could not say whether they were what living beings would in their place appear to be or not; but they appeared to me so full and so lifelike and so life-size that I could not understand why I could not feel them with my hands such as I beheld them with my eyes.

There was an extraordinary brightness about the whole gable of the chapel, and it was observed by several who were passing along the road at the time.

I remained there altogether about an hour, and when I came there first I thought I would never leave it. I would not have gone so soon as I did, but that I considered that the figures and that brightness would continue there always, and that on coming back I would again behold them.

I continued to repeat the rosary on my beads while there, and I felt great delight and pleasure in looking at the Blessed Virgin. I could think of nothing else while there but giving thanks to God repeating my prayers."

CATHERINE MURRAY

"I am living at Knock; I was staying at my grandmother's.

I followed my aunt and uncle to the chapel.

I then saw the likeness of the Blessed Virgin and that of St. Joseph and St. John, as I learned from those that were around about where I was.

I saw them fully twenty minutes or thirty minutes."

JOHN CURRY

The child says he saw the images, beautiful images, the Blessed Virgin and St. Joseph.

He could state no more than that he saw the fine images and the light, and heard the people talk of them, and went upon the wall to see the nice things and the lights.

JUDITH CAMPBELL

"I live at Knock; I remember the evening and night of the 21st August last.

Mary Byrne called at my house about eight o'clock on that evening, and asked me to come and see the great sight at the chapel.

I ran up with her to the place, and I saw outside the chapel, at the gable of the sacristy facing the south, three figures representing St. Joseph, St. John and the Blessed Virgin Mary; also an altar, and the likeness of a lamb on it, with a cross at the back of the lamb.

I saw a most beautiful crown on the brow or head of the Blessed Virgin. Our Lady was in the centre of the group, a small height above the other two; St. Joseph to her right, and bent towards the Virgin; St. John, as we were led to call the third figure, was to the left of the Virgin, and in his left hand he held a book; his right hand was raised with the first and second fingers closed, and the forefinger and middle finger extended as if he were teaching.

The night came on, and it was very wet and dark.

There was a beautiful light shining around the figures or likenesses that we saw.

I went within a foot of them; none of us spoke to them; we believed they were St. Joseph and St. John the Evangelist, because some years ago, statues of St. Joseph and of the Evangelist were in the chapel at Knock.

All the figures were in white or in a robe of silver-like whiteness; St. John wore a small mitre.

Though it was raining, the place in which the figures appeared was quite dry."

MARGARET BYRNE

"I, Margaret Byrne, live near Knock chapel; I am a sister to Mary Byrne, who has seen the vision.

I remember the night of the 21st of August; I left my own house at half past seven o'clock, and we went to the chapel and locked it; I came out to return home; I saw something luminous or bright at the south gable, but it never entered my head that it was necessary to see or inquire what it was; I passed by and went home.

Shortly after, about eight o'clock, my niece, Catherine Murray, called me out to see the Blessed Virgin and the other saints that were standing at the south gable of the chapel.

I went out then, and ran up to see what was to be seen.

I there beheld the Blessed Virgin with a bright crown on her head, and St. Joseph to her right, his head inclined a little towards Our Blessed Lady, and St. John the Evangelist to her left, eastwards, holding in his left hand a book of the gospels, and his right hand raised the while, as if in the attitude of preaching to the people who stood before him at the ditch.

The Virgin appeared with hands uplifted as if in prayer, with eyes turned towards heaven, and wearing a lustrous crown.

I saw an altar there; It was surrounded with a bright light, nay, with a light at times sparkling, and so, too, were the other figures which were similarly surrounded."

DOMINICK BYRNE (Senior)

"I live at Knock; I remember the evening of the 21st August; my cousin, Dominick Byrne, came to see us at about eight o'clock p.m., and called me to see the vision of the Blessed Virgin Mary and other saints at the south gable of the chapel.

I went with him. When I reached the south side of the chapel we saw the image of the Blessed Virgin Mary, having her hands uplifted, and her eyes turned up towards heaven, as if in prayer, and she was dressed in a white cloak.

To her right I saw St. Joseph, and on her left St. John, just as the other persons had told me before I came.

I saw an altar there, and figures representing saints and angels traced or carved on the lower part of it.

The night was dark and raining, and yet these images, in the dark night, appeared with bright lights as plain as under the noon-day sun.

At the time it was pitch dark and raining heavily, and yet there was not one drop of rain near the images.

There was a mitre on St. John's head, nearly like that which a bishop wears.

I was there for only one quarter of an hour. At the time I was there, five other persons were in it with me, looking on at the apparition.

All the figures appeared clothed in white. The whiskers on St. Joseph were an iron grey. The Blessed Virgin had on a white cloak.

The reason I had for calling the third figure St. John is because some saw his statue or his likeness at Lecanvey parish chapel."

JOHN DURKAN

One of the three who accompanied young Hill.

His testimony is the same as that given by each of the Byrnes. *